Preparing for LIFE

How to Help One's Children Become Mature and Responsible Adults

Dr Muhammad Abdul Bari

KUBE
PUBLISHING

Preparing for Life: How to help one's children to become mature and responsible adults

First published in England by
Kube Publishing Ltd
Markfield Conference Centre, Ratby Lane,
Markfield, Leicestershire, LE67 9SY,
United Kingdom
Tel: +44 (0) 1530 249230
Email: info@ kubepublishing.com
Website: www.kubepublishing.com

Copyright © Muhammad Abdul Bari 2022 All rights reserved.
The right of Muhammad Abdul Bari to be identified as the author of this work has been asserted by him in accordance with the Copyright, Designs and Patents Act, 1988.

CIP data for this book is available from the British Library.

ISBN: 978-1-84774-186-8 *Paperback*
ISBN: 978-1-84774-187-5 Ebook

Cover Design by: Jannah Haque
Typeset by: Nasir Cadir
Printed by: Elma Basim, Turkey

Contents

Introduction

Modern life has brought with it many opportunities as well as several challenges. Complex social issues are continuously emerging in families and communities. While technological progress has made life much easier and the world is becoming ever smaller, people are also suffering from the onus of being too engrossed in electronic gadgets to the detriment of a normal life and direct human communication.

The mass introduction of smartphones and the spread of the internet are keeping people incredibly busy with social media. While technological devices have helped to enhance people's education and entertainment, they have also created an information overload and heightened a culture of individualism, self-indulgence and consumerism. Young children are often left alone, for various reasons, with smartphones or iPads becoming their constant friends. As parents are getting busier, these devices become like nannies for some little children. Experts are warning that, if unsupervised and overused, these devices can have a harmful effect on young brains. The easy access to pornography and extremist materials is also a real concern for parents, as they are a danger to their natural growth and safety.

Reduced human contact with young people is becoming a source of great worry. In fact, human interaction in today's world among people living under the same roof has significantly diminished. People are always in a hurry, with little time to think, just as they are increasingly becoming loners. They hardly have time for others, be it their families, neighbourhoods or communities.

The family, with what it entails of love and sharing and caring, has always been the bedrock of human society. But this institution has been weakened in recent decades in developed societies and elsewhere. The fast increasing lack of interaction among family members is widening the generational and cultural gaps between the young and the old. The rise in mental health problems, anti-social behaviour and violence is costing people socially and economically.

It is the responsibility of the adults in the family and community to redress this growing imbalance in people's lives; they must keep on building and strengthening their families and neighbourhoods. People cannot afford to succumb to the pressures of life's grinding machine and inhibit their children's physical, mental and emotional development. They must find enough time for their families and raise their children, proactively and creatively, as decent human beings and good citizens.

In these days of growing social tension, economic inequality and political uncertainty as well as increasing intolerance, identity confusion and lack of compassion towards one another it is one's added responsibility to invest in one's children's upbringing and their overall wellbeing. One's children are one's future and trust (Arabic: *Amānah*), they need to be reared and cared for effectively in order for them to be well-equipped to create a better world.

Faith is in a flux in developed, secular and pluralist societies. Some people consider it to be of no value while others have become dogmatic and insular due to the faith they cling to, but many are simply confused. Universal human values and the teachings of different faiths have always provided people with a moral anchor and spiritual solace in the past and they have the ability to do so in the future.

As a civic activist in communities and a teacher in inner city state schools, particularly in the East End of London since the mid-1980s, I have been a keen observer of young people growing up with economic difficulties and social deprivation. I have observed how parents, communities and religious institutions try their best to raise their children with growing constraints amidst real-life challenges. Nowadays, an increasing number of people is becoming fearful of other potential pitfalls relating to their children such as sexual exploitation and radicalisation.

As a behaviour-specialist teacher in Tower Hamlets, I started running parenting courses, since the late 1990s, first on the internet, and then I ran a culturally sensitive course: *Strengthening Families, Strengthening Communities*. Later on, in the mid-2000s, I developed my own *Building Families* course that I have been occasionally running in Britain and some other global cities, which I kept improving on. A few years ago, when I took an early retirement from teaching, I launched a social enterprise, *AmanaParenting Ltd*. The *Building Families* course is about developing a whole child within the family and community contexts in a pluralist society, but with an ethos of inclusivity and an emphasis on the universal values of faith.

This book is the outcome of my long experience in working with families and young people, particularly those of Muslim persuasion, in an increasingly secularised society. Post-7/7 Britain has put British Muslims at the sharp end of serious challenges, such as higher levels of prejudice, discrimination and Islamophobia. At the same time, the Muslim community has huge opportunities to perform better with its educational and economic achievements and also to flourish by working with others for a better Britain. This book is a humble reminder to parents about multi-faceted parenting to help their children prepare for life with the ethos of universal human and Islamic values.

1

Raising one's 'little angels' as God's stewards on earth

Anewborn baby is a bundle of joy and a treasure in any family; a little angel sought after by parents, especially mothers. This 'love' comes following pain, after a nine-month long pregnancy which can only be experienced by women. That is why the mother's position is higher than that of the father's in all religious and cultural traditions. 'Paradise lies at the feet of the mothers,'[1] said Islam's Prophet (peace and blessings be upon him) Women have to be particularly careful about their own health, food habits and lifestyle during pregnancy.

Pregnancy is a 'sacrifice' that some women avoid making in today's consumerist culture because of their busy lives and individualistic frames of mind. But this unique experience to feel and see a living being growing inside their bodies must be thrilling. A woman's life changes

---

1   *Sunan al-Nasā'ī.* 3104

irreversibly from the moment she learns that she is pregnant. She carries the growing foetus until the painful delivery of the baby after about 40 weeks of pregnancy. The nurturing of the baby through a long process including the weaning period which happens after about two years, and then raising the child to adolescence is hugely demanding but it is also blissful. It takes a long time for human babies to become adults!

Once the baby is born, its parents can face tremendous difficulties, due to their irresistible love and the sheer pressure that ensues from dealing with their tiny little 'bundle of joy' that only knows how to demand. Just learning to take care of the little one physically, feeding and nappy-changing for instance, can be overwhelming. The parents' routine changes and they sleep less and insufficient rest can cause fatigue and post-natal depression in mothers. In two-parent families, the fathers help the mothers in looking after their newborn babies; in one-parent families, single parents learn how to manage on their own. Extended family members may provide help, if they are around but eventually life gradually becomes normal.

The demands that come with newborn babies also bring with them their own joy. Babies have a magnetic attraction because of their innocent looks, smiles and cooing sounds. Their total dependence on adults proffer on the parents worth and importance in life. Whatever their babies' demands are, the presence of the parents, particularly the mothers, provides physical closeness, love and security, which babies need most in their early days.

As babies grow, there is a need to adopt a gradual and natural 'programme' for their independence. This requires careful planning and positive parenting throughout all the stages of childhood; basic parenting 'skills' are essential.

Babies know naturally how to communicate and, as they grow older, they also learn 'techniques' to relate meaningfully to the world. They gradually recognise their mothers, fathers and other members of the family. They see, hear, observe, respond and keep on learning.

Countless pieces of information pile up in their brains which tend to overwhelm their understanding of the meaning of the world. However, all this contributes to building their unique personalities.

Babies are dependent but they are not ignorant or totally helpless. They can express themselves when they are happy, hungry, tired or in pain. They signal all these with their smiles, cries or body movements. Parents must take their young children's physical wellbeing safety, physical cleanliness, immunisation, etc. very seriously just as they must take care of the emotional, spiritual and intellectual aspects of their upbringing. In this formative period of a human being's journey on earth, the newborn child must have a strong grounding in all areas of life.

Newborn babies need constant company. They like to be rocked and talked to. Mothers are at the forefront of this closeness. The first two years in the life of a child is crucial in his or her rearing. The mother's milk is vital in the early stage of a child's life, not only because it is highly nutritious, but also due to the close bonding that breastfeeding creates between the mother and her baby. A baby should not be deprived of the mother's milk unless she is required to take certain drugs. Breastfeeding should continue until the baby is around two years old, according to the Islamic tradition.

Parents learn to deal with their babies by watching and listening to them and by observing their reactions. The babies' range of signals is limited, so parents need to make an extra effort to ensure that their babies recognise their signals. It would be unfortunate if mothers were tempted to stop fulfilling their basic duties before a close bond with their babies is secured. Unless absolutely necessary, mothers are advised in many cultures not to let their babies be raised by minders or nannies. Many developed countries now allow longer maternal and paternal leave from work. One thing that must not be allowed to creep into parents' minds is that the rearing of children is an inferior job, compared to working in the outside world.

Nurturing babies requires time and attention, especially after birth. Parenting, thus, requires careful noticing, interpreting and communicating with the babies as well as responding to their various needs – physical, emotional and mental. As babies grow, their demands on their parents change. As soon as the parents learn the delicate art of responding to their demands, they suddenly realise that their babies have turned into toddlers, and then into infants. Parents have to be creative and adapt themselves such that they are able to handle their children in their different phases of growth. Spending quality time with children, sometime[s] one-to-one, and putting them to bed and reading to them 'bed time stories' are good practices that help in the upbringing of children.

Babies like to play and put things in their mouths, nose and ears. As such, all dangerous items, small or big, should be kept out of their reach. They should not be left unsupervised when such items are within reach. All parents must learn a few basic rules of first aid and use common sense at times of emergency. The demands of looking after young children are ever changing and the pressure on parents varies. This requires extra patience and creativity from parents to be able to take care of their active toddler.

Things become more challenging when young children start going to nursery and come across other people, both infants and adults. This is the time when parents and adults need to be more innovative when dealing with them. At this stage, children's physical activity increases as does their quest for knowledge. The best thing for parents at this stage in their children's development is to play, have fun and allow them to 'learn through having fun'. According to the Islamic tradition, the upbringing of children consists of three stages: the first seven years are about engaging them in physical activities and letting them learn through play; the second seven years are about instructing them; and the following seven years are about being friendly with them and mentoring them wisely.

Children have sharp memories and the ability to memorise nursery rhymes or religious texts well. While parents should take advantage of this, children should not be coerced to memorise; they should be helped to develop the power of thinking that challenges their minds. The rise of nations has always been through the promotion of creative thinking and their downfall was invariably due to the absence in their midst of creative thinking. Providing children with thinking skills is therefore essential, and this includes helping them to develop personal, social, visual, linguistic, scientific and philosophical intelligence. 'Your mind is like a parachute. It only works if it is open,' says a common proverb.

Children are naturally curious and they should be encouraged to be so. They will think and ask questions about many things including the meaning of life. Curiosity sharpens their minds and gives them information processing, reasoning and creative skills. 'Every child is born a genius',[2] says Albert Einstein.

Children should be guided to consume healthy foods that have sufficient nutritional benefits, to remain physically active and to engage in intelligent games. A happy life depends on a balanced physical, emotional and mental growth. In these days of permissive society and consumerist culture, young children could easily be glued to a TV or computer or, even more so, to their smartphones. Uncontrolled use of these gadgets could insulate the children's minds from the wider world and isolate them from the people around them. In addition to making children physically inactive, these gadgets can turn them into dull and socially passive persons for their whole lives.

Children are born with many natural skills, and some may be specifically gifted with a particular one. Parents and teachers need to explore this in children and help them to excel if they have particular skills.

As parents wield an overwhelming influence on their young children, some may be 'possessive' and assert too much control on their young

2   http://www.accessncwage.com/beststeps/Beststep.cfm?bs=66.

ones. This is likely to inhibit the creativity of children. Having balance in life is vital. The best parents are those who give their children a good education, instil in them excellent manners and, at the same time, help them to develop the ability to think and be innovative.

The need to invest in one's children

From the perspective of faith, particularly the Islamic faith, children are a gift from God. Hence, investing in one's children or raising them well is the wisest thing that parents can do. The Islamic faith is intransigent regarding monotheism (Arabic: *Tawḥīd*) and insists on building positive individual and social character traits in its adherents. Chapter 31 of the Qur'ān mentions a wise father (Luqmān) who advised his son to adhere to monotheism and the core ritual of prayer as well as leading a righteous life on earth by enjoining good and forbidding evil, being humble and moderate and not being loud-mouthed. Reminders such as these are used by believing parents to raise their children as good human beings wherever they may be. In one of the seminal advice on parenting, the Prophet Muhammad (peace and blessings be upon him) said to his Companions: 'The best gift to children from parents is their correct training.' (Al-Tirmidhī)

British Muslims have got a demographic asset within their community: the high proportion of their young people. According to the 2011 census, the Muslim community is younger than the overall population, with 33% of the Muslim population below the age of 15 (compared to the national average of 19% for the same age range) and 48% below the age of 24 (compared to the national average of 31% for the same age range). The median age of the Muslim population is 25 years, compared to the overall population's median age of 40 years.[3] This can be a strategic asset for Britain.

Raising children in an age of anxiety

Contemporary Britain, like many developed western countries, is going through social challenges such as economic inequality, intolerance, Islamophobia, discrimination and extremism as well as anxieties and confusions which are the consequences of modern life. The globalisation of individualism, the sexualisation and commercialisation of life are issues that also affect all members of British society. It is obvious that in an amoral social environment, more impressionable young people may succumb to social pressure and adopt lifestyles that are often inappropriate or unacceptable to the teachings of their faiths. In a rights-based society, people have the right to choose anything if it is not harmful to society or against the law of the land. So, faith communities have to inculcate proactively their religious and spiritual ethos in their children with positive self-esteem so that they grow confidently with their multiple identities in a pluralist environment.[4]

---

3   https://www.mcb.org.uk/wp-content/uploads/2015/02/MCBCensusReport_2015.pdf

4   See, My *Race, Religion & Muslim Identity in Britain*, Claritas Books 2004, 2007, 2018 and *Identity & Violence: The Illusion of Destiny*, byf Amartya Sen, Penguin Books, 2006.

Isolation and ghettoization for any group or community are dangerous and inhibit overall social progress.

No country is perfect in dealing with its diverse citizens, but Britain has an edge over many developed countries in its pluralism and equal opportunities. There are issues of often unfair political and media pressures on the Muslim community but, in some areas of life, such as Britain's high-performing Third Sector, Muslim voluntary humanitarian works have been shining for some time. This has been possible thanks to the dedicated involvement of young Muslims, particularly the community's burgeoning professional section.

It is important that Muslim parents and the community invest in their children's education and character building in a more planned way. Young Muslims have better potentials to expand their knowledge and contribute better towards a more tolerant and respectful society.

Here are a few challenging areas that Muslim parents should be particularly aware of in raising and mentoring their children with the ethos of their faith in a modern secular society.

a) Children's overall wellbeing

In September 2006, the children's charity, *The Children's Society*, commissioned *The Good Childhood Inquiry* 'to renew society's understanding of modern childhood and to inform, improve and inspire all our relationships with children.' I was invited to join this first independent national inquiry chaired by Professor Judy Dunn of King's College, London. The result of this inquiry was the report: *A Good Childhood: Searching for values in a competitive age*, published in early 2009.

In recent decades, Britain's young people have not been faring well in their overall wellbeing, compared to other developed countries. In the 2007 UNICEF report[5] on children's wellbeing, which included Behaviours and Risks, in 21 rich countries, Britain came at the bottom

---

5   https://www.unicef.org/media/files/ChildPovertyReport.pdf

of the list. After many years working with communities and inner city secondary schools in London, I have observed that many in our society have a tendency to reproach young people for their ill-manners and anti-social behaviour. It is true that there are some poorly behaved young people who individually, or through their involvement in gangs, wander aimlessly and behave in an anti-social way. There are also classrooms in some areas where teachers feel unable to deal with pupils' behaviours. But it is also true that, as a whole, young people are probably not valued, encouraged or respected enough; there is a habit in society of stigmatising young people. 'If we demonise an entire generation, we'll pay the price,'[6] says one academic.

Sadly, some young Muslims, especially in inner cities, are falling prey to the lure of modern life. Even young people from the known conservative Pakistani and Bangladeshi backgrounds (these two communities constitute over two-thirds of the British Muslim population) are affected by some practices that are antithetical to their faith and cultural norms. London Assembly published a report in 2009 which revealed that 'young people from Muslim communities, whose Islamic faith forbids alcohol, are now drinking far more - girls now are as bad as boys for underage drinking.'[7] Only a generation ago most people in the Muslim community could proudly declare they have nothing to do with this practice. But this is no longer the case; many Muslim parents are now worried about this. Not only can addictions negatively affect the educational achievement of the community, they also hinder its social progress. Worst of all, drug and alcohol can lead many to crime. Many young Muslim prisoners, disproportionately higher compared to any other community, are known to have committed criminal offences due to addiction problems.

6   http://www.telegraph.co.uk/comment/personal-view/5007885/The-fear-of-young-people-damages-us-all.html
7   https://www.theguardian.com/society/2009/jun/16/underage-drinking-girls-pakistani-bangladeshi

Delinquency is often seen as a symptom of rebelliousness during puberty and adolescence. However, delinquent behaviour before or after puberty may also be a sign that a child is emotionally disturbed because of issues such as poor parenting or violence at home. Young people tend to get along with their peers and follow role models. As they are generally impressionable, they may have a tendency to rebel against the status quo. In the absence of a loving relationship with their parents and firm discipline at home, some youth may turn to delinquent behaviour and can eventually resort to antisocial or even criminal activities.

Muslim parents need to be aware of what is going on in their children's world and discuss juvenile issues with warmth and a sense of urgency at home and in community institutions. They must devote quality time and exert extra efforts with their own beloved children and creatively help them grow as good human beings.

b) Bullying and hate crimes

Bullying in the form of verbal harassment, intimidation or coercion is a worrying phenomenon in many schools. It destroys the self-esteem of the victims and can cause long term psychological problems in them. Bullies tend to target those who seem to be different or not like 'one of them'. Loners, socially passive children or children of minority groups may easily become targets of bullying. Both the bully and the victim lack self-esteem. Often, bullies have been victims of abuse themselves, which they deal with through bullying others.

By law, all schools must have clear behaviour and anti-bullying policies, with robust implementation strategies. In recent times, cyber bullying that is when a child is tormented, threatened, harassed, humiliated, embarrassed or otherwise targeted by another child through the Internet, interactive and digital technologies or mobile phones has multiplied in worrying proportions. Whether physical or cyber, some forms of bullying such as theft, violence or assault, repeated harassment or intimidation (for example name calling, threats and abusive phone calls, emails or text messages) and hate crimes are illegal and should be reported to the police.[8]

Britain has a long history of accommodating people from other parts of the world at different times of its history, as it did with the French Huguenots, European Jews, Catholics, Blacks and Asians. Some communities suffered racism and hate crime after their arrival in the UK; hate crimes against Muslims significantly rose after the 7/7 terrorist attacks in London. Since then the community has suffered negative media portrayals that has exacerbated physical attacks on Muslim individuals and religious institutions. Racism and hate crimes have worsened[9] for all minority communities, including Muslims, in the aftermath of the vote for Brexit on 23 June 2016.

Muslim children are more susceptible to be the target of bullying and racism because of their names, dress and culture; Muslim girls are even more so. The prevailing atmosphere of mistrust vis-à-vis Muslims is affecting their young people in schools and other public places. At the same time, they also face discrimination in the labour market.

c) Preserving childhood innocence

The early sexualisation of young people is having a negative impact on their innocence and balanced growth. Social media, TV commercials, tabloids and erotic magazines as well as online pornographic materials are to blame for such sexualisation. This puts huge pressures on the young and often impressionable minds. It has also an unwholesome influence on their attitude towards the opposite sex from an early age. Eroticism in adverts, films and the media is provocative to adolescents and creates unnecessary pressures on them. School inspectors from Ofsted often come across inappropriate sexual behaviour among

---

8   https://www.gov.uk/bullying-at-school/the-law
9   http://www.bbc.co.uk/news/uk-politics-37640982

children, including even primary school pupils[10], that is worrying to parents. Lifestyles have also changed over the past few decades. The rise in family breakdown and domestic violence across the board affect children's lives and education.

Children grow into men and women and, thus, they are a precious national asset; their future role in society is promising. But paedophilia, the crime of using young children for sexual gratification or financial profit, treats them ignominiously. The horrendous crime of grooming young girls by sexual predators has been exposed in recent times.

To many parents and social scientists, this unfair and unkind pressure on young people can hamper their natural growth and destroy their childhood innocence. Of course, children should be given age-appropriate knowledge and life-experience in a sensitive and positive manner so that they are better equipped in life. But many people are fearful that exposure to insensitive or suggestive materials and the lack of adult supervision may be gateways to conforming to an indulgent life during children's innocent and preparatory stage of life. Underage sexual activity, resulting in teenage pregnancy, is a serious concern.

Young people in religious traditions, particularly the Islamic one, are considered as gifts from God. Parents and society have an obligation to raise, educate and prepare them with life skills in a safe environment. Their overall wellbeing and safeguard from sexual exploitation and extremism are vital. In an open, civil and democratic society, people have multiple life choices within the broad remit of the law. So, parents in religious communities are expected to instil in their children a firm attitude and teach them to engage in sex only in the context of marriage at an appropriate age.

---

10   https://www.theguardian.com/education/2009/jun/23/sexualised-pupils-primary-schools-ofsted

The need for a better generation

As the Muslim community has come under pressure in recent years, parents are obviously worried about the safety of their children in schools and the streets. It is not easy to tackle social challenges, especially in the context of the weak socio-economic condition of the Muslim community. This cannot be done by one group or a community in isolation; society as a whole needs to work together. There needs to be a joint approach and action from people in authority and civil society, including the Muslim community itself, to combat the current impasse between the Muslim community and the wider society. Running away from the real problem or working through piecemeal methods is ineffective.

But the community itself – its social and religious leaders, community activists and young professionals – must work hard to take control of their destiny. The Islamic faith expects its adherents to excel (Arabic: *Iḥsān*) in whatever they do. It is important for parents and concerned adults to assess the situation and come up with realistic policies to invest in their younger ones so that they may flourish in a generally meritocratic Britain.

a) Create a positive family environment

A loving, stable and happy family environment is essential for the healthy growth of children. On the other hand, a family torn apart by neglect, abuse or violence is a nightmare for them. In a mystical poem, the 13th-century Persian Muslim mystic and scholar, Rumi, used the metaphor of the grave to depict the dysfunctional or broken family:

- A child bitterly cried besides his father's coffin,
- 'Why are they taking you to such a narrow house,
- So dark and cold, with no carpets, no doors,
- And no way out!
- With no smell of cooking, no kind neighbours,

- Why are they taking you to such a lonely place?"
- A boy walking with his father overheard the child's lament
- And asked, "Father, are they taking the corpse to our house?"[11]

In order to create and sustain a stable and sound family environment, where children can flourish, parents have to be emotionally and mentally prepared for this; they have to address the issue of parenting seriously and creatively. Children face significant challenges when they reach puberty, with abrupt changes in their bodies' chemistry and emotional state. This is also the time when they move to secondary schools whereby their material world suddenly expands. Caring and careful parents must be able to comprehend these changes in their children's world and their parenting style needs to be adapted to this reality.

Education is the gateway to success for any nation and, fortunately, British Muslim children have come a long way in their educational achievement over the decades. Whether in state schools, independent Muslim or mainstream private schools, parental responsibility regarding the educational and social well-being of children must remain constant; schools can only do their best to help in this respect. Parents should also take responsibility regarding their children's Islamic education at home or in the evening or weekend supplementary schools in mosques. Thankfully, many local councils now support mosques by providing expert and professional advice, particularly in the area of children protection and safeguard.

Educationalists in the state and private sectors should be in the forefront of addressing the educational and emotional needs of young children in society. It is encouraging that an increasing number of Muslim professionals are now coming forward to run supplementary classes in local communities. Additionally, the emergence of the Muslim community, as a congregation of individuals hailing from the

---

11   Rumi's *Little Book of Life: The Garden of the Soul, the Heart and the Spirit*. Please provide the publication details and page number of this quote.

four corners of the world, highlights the importance of adult education for its overall progress. Mosques and community centres should take the initiative to promote the local people's life-long learning, which will help in developing their parenting skills in contemporary Britain.

At a time when slick social media, easily available through electronic gadgets, are keeping children busy while decreasing their interaction with their near and dear ones, parents have a seminal role in keeping the close bond between family members. Planned parenting, such as spending quality time with children, using positive discipline techniques and organising family and community events, help to prevent young people from falling prey to loneliness, isolation and individualism, all of which are modern malaises. This will positively impact on the youngsters' school discipline and educational performance.

b) Helping children reach adulthood with values and life skills

As children reach adolescence they need effective support from those around them in families, schools, youth centres and mosques. Due to the current political climate of anti-Muslim rhetoric, young Muslim adults today are expected to work twice as hard as others. They should therefore be equipped with better skills of communication, technical knowhow and decision making in public life. They should be absolutely confident of the compatibility of their religious principles with the universal human values of a pluralist society.

Young people are amazingly creative and energetic; they need positive role models and empathetic mentoring in order to grow as future leaders. They need sympathetic support to understand their place in Britain so as to play their positive role in society. Home is the best place to sow in children the seeds of education, enterprise and human goodness. Religious institutions, youth centres and community groups should then provide them with the necessary added support to flourish in life.

Like other youths, young Muslims are smart and full of potential. They need guidance and assistance to choose the career of their choice in order to earn a living respectably. However, it has been observed that there is a tendency in some Muslim communities to cajole young people to choose only a few specific careers, such as accountancy or medicine; some Asian parents, including Muslims, are over-enthusiastic in persuading their children to become doctors.[12] This is obviously a matter of choice within a family context for whatever reasons, whether material such as job prospects and security or something else. But a community should also think positively of diversifying the career choices of its young people for the greater overall benefit of the nation.

The other important area of guidance for young Muslims is helping them find suitable marriage partners at the right age, as marriage at an appropriate age is recommended in the Islamic tradition (*Sunnah*). In recent times, there has been a trend among young Muslims to delay marriage; the situation appears to be even worse among Muslim women.[13] This is a real worry for many parents. Finding a suitable marriage partner is not easy in real life, as expectations are generally high in both sexes. However, there appears to be an increasing lack of compromise in marriageable young people due to several factors, including the negative impact of materialism. Community institutions should build support networks that provide pre-marital advice and guidance to young people. Imams and community elders should come up with practical steps to ensure the success of the institution of marriage in their community.

Social challenges within the Muslim communities are becoming more complex with the passage of time. It is vital that parents and other adults exert serious but wise efforts to inculcate the universal human

---

12 https://www.theguardian.com/commentisfree/2016/jun/08/forcing-your-child-to-become-a-doctor-could-be-the-worst-parenting-decision-you-make

13 https://www.theguardian.com/commentisfree/belief/2012/jan/18/british-muslim-women-marriage-struggle

values of justice, fairness and equality in their youngsters so that they grow with a strong moral anchor and a sense of responsibility towards others. This can be achieved through a higher level of community awareness and positive support mechanisms. Good practices abound in the community across the country; they need to be shared in earnest. More creative initiatives with a joined-up approach can ensure that no young Muslim in the community falls through the net.

3

Love and care at the heart of raising children

For most parents, the birth of a child is a euphoric and ecstatic moment. It is a high point as well as a fulfilment in their life journeys. One can only appreciate such a feeling when one is blessed with a child. The tiny human being coming out of the mother's secured womb, a totally vulnerable lump of flesh and blood creates a magnetic attractions towards the child and the mother an father.

A child is the fruit of love between two human beings. For people who have religious faith, such a life starts from God's love for His creation. Love, kindness, compassion and harmony are at the heart of biological continuity. One of the fascinating things about humans, and even some animal species, is the immeasurable and indescribable love they have for their little ones. Men and women are created as a pair in this world: the love between them is the essence of human continuity. Love is the fountainhead of passionate feelings and emotions. It is expressed and manifested in the family through mercy, compassion and care.

The natural demand of love seems to give freedom to one's child; on the other hand, such a natural demand of care requires discipline. Love and care are as intertwined with each other as freedom and discipline are. All these are inherently embedded in human nature. Freedom without limits and discipline without love are detrimental to children as they are to all people.

That's what makes parenting a challenging but joyful experience. Once a child is born, the parents' priorities and lifestyle naturally change or get readjusted. An unquestionable sense of responsibility fills the air at home. Holding a newborn baby, as it cries for the first time, is the most wonderful and radiant experience for any parent. The first skin-to-skin contact with the baby can be ecstatic. The parents' tender hug of their baby says to it: 'you are the most loved one on earth; we are here for you'.

Parenting is for the child's sake: from the embryonic stage in the mother's womb, gradually developing into a fully-dependent tiny human being and then growing into adulthood. Parenting is essentially an investment for the successful future of a loving offspring – a very long time in the future indeed. Once again, love is at the heart of the experience of parenting!

'If your plan is for one year, plant rice; if your plan is for ten years, plant trees; if your plan is for one hundred years, educate children,' said the Chinese thinker and social philosopher, Confucius.

The Prophet of Islam (peace and blessings be upon him) is reported to have said, 'When the son of Adam passes away, he is cut off from his deeds except for three things: an ongoing charity, good knowledge that benefits others, and a righteous child who makes supplication for him.'[14] There are numerous other words of wisdom on the need for effective parenting.

Experts have talked about different styles of parenting – authoritarian, indulgent, neglectful and authoritative – and their impacts on children and their advice for parents is to be authoritative.

---

14 *Ṣaḥīḥ Muslim*, 1631.

The essence of authoritative parenting is love. Some have used the term 'positive parenting' or 'rational parenting' for this style of parenting, but whatever one may call it, it is 'common sense parenting'.

Children need unconditional love, support, guidance and positive encouragement to grow in a balanced way in order to unleash their potentials. They also need to experience the realities of life as well as the challenges and dynamics that affect their lives and place in society. They need to face the realities and challenges of life in order to develop their self-esteem and grow so that their potentials flourish. Parents reward or sanction their children because of their limitless love for them. The love of parents for their children continues as long as they live.

Each parent needs to build an intuitive and emotional bond with each of his or her children. For this, it is vital that a parent spends plenty of quality time with each child regularly and consistently. This is vital in every stage of the child's development, particularly during the onset and turbulent years of adolescence. In the family where one parent is unable to fulfil this, for whatever reason, the other parent should try to compensate for it.

It is also vital that the child becomes central to the family, or extended family, where the ethos of sharing and caring, compromise and sacrifice are practised and promoted. No matter how busy the parents may be, it is essential to have age-appropriate communication and continuous discussions with children in the family context. It is also an absolute necessity to show a consistent parental behaviour with children and other members of the family: children must understand their parents. Parental consistency is vital for the development of their self-confidence. Inconsistency, emotional outbursts and violence in the family destroy the innocence of children and future adults.

Children need some structure and discipline for their balanced growth in life. Parents with good routines in life help their children enormously. Home is children's first school, but a family environment must be relaxed and should not be like a school or workplace. A flexible, but broadly agreed-upon, boundary is required. It is also beneficial to take advantage of local resources from family friends, the neighbourhood and community. As children grow and go to nursery or school, parental interest in their educational and social needs, especially in their early development period, is vital.

Parenting is a generational and inter-generational task for the development and sustenance of stable, peaceful and successful societies. Through positive parenting, the family plays the role of a nursery, school and university, and produces conscientious and humane generations. Parenting, unpaid and often unrecognised, is definitely a demanding task but it is one of life's core tasks. It is challenging but thoroughly enjoyable, rewarding and adventurous. To people of faith, parenting is ever important for this life and the life to come, as children are an '*Amānah*' and '*Fitnah*', i.e. a 'trust' and 'test'.

Parenting needs creative thinking, strategic planning, full commitment and a great deal of compromise. As leaders, mentors and teachers of children, parents are the creators of new worlds.

On the authority of Abū Hurayrah who said: 'I heard Allah's Apostle saying, "Allah has divided mercy into one-hundred parts and He kept ninety-nine parts with Him and sent down one part on the earth, and because of that one part, His creations are merciful towards one another, so that even the mare lifts up its hoofs away from its baby animal to avoid trampling it."' (*Ṣaḥīḥ al-Bukhārī*)

On the authority of 'Umar ibn Al-Khaṭṭāb who said: 'Some captives of war were brought before the Prophet and, behold! There was a woman amongst them who was breastfeeding any child she found among the captives. She would press the child to her chest and nurse it (she had lost her child but later found him). Seeing this, the Prophet said to us, "Do you think that this lady can throw her son in the fire?" We replied, "No, if she has the power not to throw it (in the fire)." The Prophet then said, "Allah is more merciful to His slaves than this lady is to her son."' (*Ṣaḥīḥ al-Bukhārī*)

4

Enthusing good reading habits in the family

There are certain praiseworthy practices that indicate that a nation is successful, and one practice which stands out is the widespread habit of reading amongst its citizens. Reading guarantees these people's future with a better education which uplifts their position and dignity in the world. In a nation like this, the houses of most people would have a private library, no matter how small. Even in crowded public transport, one sees people engaged in reading; they cannot afford to remain unproductive by staying idle in their journey.

Having a reading habit is one of the best indicators of an enlightened nation. Lasting civilisations are mainly built through intellectual supremacy and not just through physical power. The Muslim civilisation was a shining example of a nation based on knowledge, ever since the early Muslims created a vibrant community based on the message of the

Qur'ān and teachings of the Prophet Muhammad (peace and blessings be upon him). The first verse revealed to the Prophet was 'Read in the name of your Lord who created.'[15] Islam left a long and permanent impact on human history.

Post-Renaissance Europe which has given birth to the 'West' is the product of its intellectual journey spurred by its encounter with Muslims. During the Middle Ages, when Europe was intellectually paralyzed and its public life was rigidly controlled by the Church, Muslim universities in the Iberian Peninsula and the Middle East were the main source of knowledge for European scholars. The contribution of Muslim scholars inspired European minds. The invention of the printing machine in 1451 CE was instrumental in passing this new-found knowledge from a few privileged elites to the masses. An inner energy and drive to explore the world ensued which led to investigation, discovery and empirical research.

Craving for knowledge in Muslim history

In his *The Islamic Civilisation*[16] a prominent Syrian scholar, Muṣṭafā Sibā'ī, mentions some fascinating stories about Muslims' reading habit. At a time when there were no publishing facilities and books were expensive for ordinary people, affluent Muslims and scholars spent their wealth to establish libraries, mostly adjacent to schools or mosques, so that everyone could read and benefit from them. Most libraries were run through endowments set up from contributions by generous people. One library in Cairo established by the Fatimid Caliphs contained about two million books!

A new 'Library Science' emerged through this process and Muslims became real bookworms. Due to their thirst for knowledge and literary taste, numerous libraries were established in most part of the Muslim

---

15 al-Alaq 96:1.
16 *The Islamic Civilisation*, by Mustafa Sibai, Awakening Publications, 2002, pp.180-192.

world. Many philanthropists spent their fortunes in establishing libraries. On the whole, public and private libraries helped Muslims' intellectual supremacy for a long period. Books and libraries connected Muslims' material progress with their spiritual quest.

Calamity befell the Muslims in the 13th century when the Mongols overran Muslim lands, burning cities and libraries in the process; this was a symptom as well as a cause of Muslim decline. The erosion of reading habits, intellectual passivity and gradual political fracture continued until a rejuvenated Europe colonized vast territories of the Muslim world. The decadence of Muslims continued during the colonial period which caused more disconnection between Muslims and the sources of knowledge; and their slumber continued until their fight for independence which most Muslim countries gained in the middle of the 20th century.

But the post-independent Muslim world failed to revive the old craving of Muslims for knowledge, mainly because of ineffective or corrupt political leaderships and weak religious scholarship. In the absence of a robust civil society, the grinding reality of illiteracy, poverty and economic stagnation overshadowed the optimism that was created during the liberation struggle of many Muslim countries. Fast forward, the post-9/11 Muslim situation has opened a Pandora's box of intractable multiple crises, particularly in the Arab world.

The importance of knowledge in Islam

God has made knowledge the criterion for the superiority of human beings over other creatures, including angels, and He bestowed knowledge on the first human being who was also the first Prophet (upon him be peace). The last Prophet, Muhammad (peace and blessings be upon him), was unlettered but he was nonetheless blessed with divine knowledge and he guided people through a model generation of highly dedicated Companions. The Qur'an is full of knowledge and reminders to people. Its verses are called '*Āyāt*' (meaning signs). The other creatures on earth are also called *Āyāt* in Arabic. Muslims are encouraged to seek knowledge by reading or encountering both these signs of God and then reflect, learn and lead their lives as stewards on this earth.

However, although mere reading of the Qur'an is rewarding, it is not enough. Muslims are required to 'study' it and understand its meanings, so that they can act on its teachings. Knowledge and understanding lead to the truth and draw one nearer to God. The following verses are precious for Muslims:

> **O my Lord! Advance me in knowledge.**
> *(*Qur'an, 20:114*)*

> **Say: Are those who know equal with those who know not?**
> *(*Qur'an, 39:9*)*

The Qur'an is a guide for people, urging them to reflect and act with rectitude. Muslims are expected to be a reading people to succeed in both worlds. The Prophet Muhammad (peace and blessings be upon him) insisted a great deal on acquiring knowledge; the following two sayings are illuminating:

> *The Prophet Muhammad (peace and blessings be upon him) said:*
> *'Seeking knowledge is obligatory for every Muslim.'*
> (Al-Tirmidhī)

> *'The superiority of the man of knowledge over the devotee is like that*
> *of the full moon over the rest of the stars. The scholars are the heirs*
> *of the Prophets, and the Prophets leave behind neither gold nor silver*
> *coins, they only leave behind knowledge, and the one who acquires it*
> *has acquired a big fortune.'*
> (Abū Dāwūd)

Empowering children with a reading habit

A nation's success or failure depends on the quality of its individuals and their feelings and commitments. The quality of an individual or group is commensurate with their reading habits, education and life-long preparation. When individuals develop a reading habit, it can be transmitted to their families, communities and societies. This in turn creates a nation with intellectual leadership and political direction.

Muslims' educational level and reading habits in Muslim majority and minority countries, such as Britain, are not satisfactory at all. The best way to overcome impoverishment and ignorance is through developing reading habits at home. The lead in this respect should come from parents at home, teachers in school and Imams in mosques. It is only through reclaiming the spirit of reading and learning that the overall Muslim situation will change positively.

The act of reading is empowering. It empowers the ordinary person; it enriches the scholar; and it gives confidence to the whole nation. Reading stimulates one's mind by giving it food for thought. It drives one to take on the challenges of real life. It develops one's mental faculty, increases one's understanding, enhances one's thinking power and imparts one with the gift of wisdom. Reading increases one's curiosity and enhances one's critical acumen. Just as a balanced diet keeps one physically active, good books keep one mentally agile and spiritually alive.

Good books are companions that never let one down. They protect one from falling into major mistakes and teach one to be more disciplined. They inspire, make life enterprising, adventurous and also enjoyable. They motivate one to work harder, inspire one to become determined in aiming high and succeeding in life. They can lift one from one's comfort zone and bring one closer to the sharpest minds of the past and present. They teach one how to express oneself and how to become a decent human being and a good citizen. One is always in conversation with books. They remain in one's mind even when one is not reading them and they give one hope when one is despondent. Good books are the source of a silent and deep power; they are essentially means of success.

But in the world of information overload, one has to pick and choose what to read. The art of skim reading is one way that enables one to read more, but one needs to read deeply when required. Like other habits in life, reading has to be based on choice. Muslims' reading should be for a life purpose in order to fill their hearts and souls; one should read materials that nourish one within and also help society. Reading, reflecting and acting should be soundly balanced. In one's limited lifespan, one cannot afford to waste time, i.e. life, by reading junk. Just as junk food is unhealthy for the body, reading trash materials is also morally and spiritually unhealthy.

Muslims must instil a good reading habit in their children. This should start early in their lives by introducing them to age-appropriate books and rewarding them for reading so that they grow up as bookworms and lovers of books.

5

Motivating one's children

One of the toughest and most challenging things regarding children of all ages is how to motivate them to do things and keep them consistently motivated. One hears so often from children, from infancy to adolescence: 'I'm bored,' 'I'm tired,' 'what's the point of doing this?' etc. This happens with almost all children at some point in their upbringing. The issue becomes more challenging when children become adolescents, with all what this entails of teenage issues that take centre stage in their lives, such as boy-girl relationships, and the ever-changing fashions and lifestyle. This can create agitation in many families, especially if these families are not stable or parental relationship is weak and parenting skills are generally poor. Parents and adults must provide a strong, moral authority and a good persuasive power to keep children interested, motivated and inspired.

Motivation and the theories behind it are very important in academic research and organisational performance. What is it that drives people to do certain things? What is it that motivates someone to do things? What keeps them going in their day-to-day life?

Many people spend their lives in the service of others, their community and society. What motivates them to do so? What drives some people to spend their time, energy and hard-earned money in helping others and engaging in the struggle for equality, social justice and political principles – and most of it, or all, for nothing in return? Is this due to an urge for personal fulfilment, a desire for fame or is it just an act of benevolence towards others? Does this urge come from one's human instinct, sympathy for others, patriotic fervour, ideological commitment, religious zeal or spiritual solace? Why do some people have this 'fire' in them, while others do not?

The issue of motivation is very complex. In psychology it is defined as the process that initiates, guides and maintains goal-oriented behaviours.[17] It is what causes one to act or 'get going'. Motivation is an inner urge that involves biological, emotional, social and cognitive forces that activate one's behaviour. Various triggers, internal and external, combine to create motivation in one. Reward and sanction are important for some; but others are motivated despite the lack of any worldly reward or sanction. John Adair, a British leadership theorist, explains "Motivation is closer in meaning to the older English concept of *motivity*: the power of initiating or producing movement. All these words – motive, motivation, motivity – come from the Latin verb 'to move'. What moves us to action may come from within or from without, or – more commonly – from some combination of inner impulse or proclivity on the one hand and outer situations or stimulation the other."

For faith-inspired people, particularly Muslims, the motivation of the believer to do good things could be the love of God, His reward or

---

17 *Leadership and Motivation: The fifty-fifty rule and the eight key principles of motivating others*, by John Adair, Kogan Page, 1990, p. 41.

sanction, His mercy or wrath, in the Hereafter. Islam, meaning 'peace' (through wilful surrender to God), expects its adherents to serve people from any background and make sacrifices for the sake of the truth and justice. Muslims throughout history were motivated by the teachings of their Prophet Muhammad (peace and blessings be upon him). For religious people, it is divine love that drives them to lead righteous lives for the benefit of humanity and stewardship on earth. Prophets were shining exemplars regarding their sacrifices for the sake of human welfare. Prophet Abraham (peace be upon him) is particularly mentioned in the Qur'an for passing God's tests, so he became His beloved and was made a leader of people.[18] Many among the Prophetic Companions and the two following generations in early Islamic history were gifted servants of humanity. Rābi'ah al-Baṣriyyah,[19] in the 8th century, was known as the "queen of saintly women" for her deep and pure love of God.

However, for ordinary people in this modern complex time, maintaining the parents' motivation and motivating children are a big challenge. Practical matters, such as struggling with one's job, managing one's family budget, raising children in an age of anxiety, etc., are exhausting; people are stressed and do often snap. But frustration, anger or despondence need the antidote of resilience, inner peace and spiritual solace to lift one's confidence. Parents should always see the "glass half full" in their children and look out for natural ways to re-energise themselves and motivate their children. The following are a few relevant guidelines for parents which should be thoughtfully and creatively applied with their children:

---

18 When Abraham's Lord tested him in certain matters he *passed the test*. He (God) said: "Indeed I am going to appoint you a leader of all people". When Abraham asked: "And is this covenant also for my descendants"? The Lord *replied*: "My covenant does not embrace the wrong doers." (Qur'an, 2:124)
19 Islamic Spirituality: Foundations, edited by Hossein Nasr, pdf version, Routledge, 2008, p. 389.

1. Building a loving relationship with one's children

A consistent loving relationship and creative guidance in building children's behaviour are vital for their natural growth as well as for motivating them. As men and women have unique and complementary features, both parents should share the joy of looking after their children and employ innovative techniques to build in them self-esteem so that they do things through their own volition. Muslim parents should remember the three seven-year phases of children's growth and act diligently to make sure their children grow as whole persons with humane qualities. Young children learn through games and play, but they need someone to oversee this so that they are always safe. Once they grow naturally and without inhibition in their first seven-year phase that may require the parents' constant commitment, children can learn better in the next seven-year phase. In the next phase, parents and teachers should be friendlier with children while providing education and guidance with real-life inspirations and examples so that children are self-motivated.

2. Parents must be role models

The adage "Example is better than precept" is universal. Obviously parents expect their children to grow as motivated individuals. For this reason, it is vital they themselves practise what they preach. Role modelling is probably the most effective way of educating children. A positive home environment in which love, respect, sharing and caring are abundant is a source of happiness for a growing child. Before being bombarded with the lifestyles of celebrities promoted in the media, children take their parents as role models. It is a great challenge for parents to adjust their everyday life and try to be role models for their children. As children grow, the mother and father can become practical role models for their adolescent daughters and sons.

3. Creating a vision

Parents are essentially leaders and one of their tasks is to raise their children in a stable and happy environment and provide them with vision in life. People are disparate in their strengths and weaknesses. Their lives are also full of challenges, but parents must remain positive and instil in their children a positive attitude. Children themselves may bring in additional challenges for their parents, but the latter should always have a positive attitude towards them. They should never undermine them due to falling in occasional misdemeanours. Being positive in life and cultivating positive features in one's children are vital ingredients in any family with a well-bonded and long-lasting relationship among its members. This is how children's self-esteem and confidence grow, and this is how children remain motivated in life.

4. Spending quality time with one's children

Children are born as a result of love and every child deserves special love and attention from both parents. Children should know, and be often reminded verbally and through body language, that they are exceptionally dear to their parents. Parenting specialists suggest that, when children reach their third year onward, both mother and father must spend every week, independently but in a planned way, regular one-to-one special times with each one of their children. Depending on the availability of parents, this could be every day, for about fifteen minutes, with pre-adolescent children, and at least for half an hour once a week with secondary school-age children. Parents should inform their children of this special parental time with each one of them. The specialist advice is that, during this time, children should be allowed to talk freely and frankly; each parent should give full attention to what his or her child says.

5. Strengthening the sense of ethnic and cultural roots in children

Children, especially as they enter adolescence, should be proudly aware but also humble about their attachment to their own family, ethnicity and cultural roots. This gives them confidence in their identity and a sense of continuity. 'To remain ignorant of things that happened before you were born is to remain a child,'[20] said Roman philosopher and politician Cicero. The people who neglect their history are like individuals who have dementia. People without a sense of belonging find it difficult to have direction in their lives. This is why, in all nations, history is one of the most important curriculum subjects in the school education system. However, children should be taught that belonging to an ethnicity, religion or cultural roots does not mean that they should lead insular lives or dislike others who are different from them. Besides being contrary to religious texts and teachings, living a parallel or ghettoized life does not only amount to self-centredness but it is also harmful for all. Human beings are like a multi-coloured flower garden where each different person complements the others to form a human garden.

---

20 https://www.goodreads.com/author/quotes/13755.Marcus_Tullius_Cicero

6

Bridging generational and cultural gaps

O ver the centuries, Europe embraced secularism and curtailed the role of organised religion in the public domain. In Britain, however, ethics and morality have their roots in its main religion, Christianity, and are still influenced by it. In post-WWII Britain, the practice of religion has increased with the arrival of many faith communities from, mainly, the Commonwealth nations which has instigated a debate on the role of religion in a secular, and increasingly atheist environment. It is in this context that the emergence of diverse Muslim communities should be considered.

Britain's Muslim community is evolving and Muslims are still arriving to the UK from war-torn countries as refugees and asylum seekers. Muslims are a group of overwhelmingly ordinary people who have similar hopes, aspirations, frustrations, failures and successes to any other people in the land. With a higher proportion of youth in their midst, they have issues relating to identity crisis amongst some of them, but they otherwise have all the potentials to succeed.

However, with the rising of educational levels in the last couple of decades and rapid technological progress in recent times, young Muslims are instituting some changes in their social attitude and cultural practices. Like the youths of other communities, they are also influenced by change-makers such as television, the internet and social media; sometimes they even set the tone of change. As direct human interaction in society is diminishing, online activities and social networking are occupying much of young people's time. Many parents, especially from the first generation immigrant population, are obviously struggling to keep pace with these changes.

Building a life-long connection with one's children is not easy. There have always been inter-generational gaps in every society at all times. But the gap between first generation parents and their techno-savvy children in Muslim communities appears to be much wider. This gap is more visible in areas such as lifestyle, fashion, musical tastes, religious practices, culture and even politics.

Due to a great religious emphasis on the family values of reciprocal care and share, the young and old tend to remain physically close whenever possible. But in the new social environment, with its economic hardship for many families, young Muslims spend less time with the adults around them, even if they happen to live under the same roof. In some cases there is some disconnection between parents and their teenage children. Scary stories of juvenile delinquency or young people wandering around in gangs frighten some elderly people, including Muslims. On the other hand, young people also feel undervalued as they are often demonised by the adult world. There is always a need for more empathy, recognition and respect for one another.

Over two thirds of British Muslims have roots in South Asian countries. For economic and other reasons, the majority lives in Britain's inner cities. Together with Muslims from other parts of the world, the community has become hugely diverse. Many are used to religious and social conservatism, but some practices are obviously cultural and not necessarily "Islamic".

Muslim culture, however different internally, has features that often converge on the nature of the family and its values, dress and modesty, an understanding of spirituality, the practice of greeting one another, food habits, celebrations, creative expressions, expectations in life, environmental views, illness and bereavement, etc. How much of this culture is being passed on to the new generations of Muslims to help them form an inclusive identity in a secular, pluralist society is a matter of continuous discussion, inside and outside the community.

However, whilst maintaining cultural uniqueness is important for an ethnic or faith community, it is vital for all citizens to be an active part of the wider society. For this to happen positively and naturally, an awareness and understanding of the mainstream society are essential. Parents' interaction with the wider society helps them to raise their children and prepare them for better citizenship. Better inclusiveness in mosques and community centres can really help the local community to be on the same wavelength regarding social integration.

Muslim children, like their peers from other communities, are exposed to all sorts of challenges and opportunities in modern life. Parents at home need to be aware of what goes on in their children's lives. They should work with teachers and imams to help their children develop with confidence in their own worth. Here is a list of some manifestations of identity[21] that most young Muslims grow up with at home - but should learn how to confidently and comfortably live with others in a diverse secular society.

---

21 *Race, Religion and Muslim Identity in Britain*, by Muhammad Abdul Bari, Renaissance Press, 2005, p. 109.

Manifestation of identity	Examples
Faith/belief	The belief system, i.e., whether and how someone believes in monotheism, the trinity, original sin, etc.
Marriage/Family	Issues regarding marriage, man–woman relationship, the extended family structure and family ethos, etc.
Appearance/clothes	Cultural and religious expressions regarding modesty and beauty, likes and dislikes, e.g., dress for men and women, beards, hairstyle.
Food/eating habits	Type of foods and drinks and how they are consumed, e.g., alcohol, pork, Halal or Kosher.
Socialisation	Visits, family gatherings, pub culture, etc.
Rituals	Prayer and prayer facilities, holidays, pilgrimage, etc.
Creative expressions	Art, calligraphy, poetry, music, dance, drama, architecture, e.g., minarets.
Celebration/entertainment	Religious, historical and national, e.g., Eid, Diwali, Hanuka, Christmas.
Verbal expressions	Vocabulary, terminology and expression.
Visits and holidays	Time and places people visit and go to on holidays.
Inter-generational interaction	Respect and sensitivity when people of different generations talk and interact.
Economic habit	Incomes, expenditures, investment, issue of ethics, e.g., interest.
Illness and bereavement	Religious and cultural requirements as well as taboos regarding them.

It may appear to some that, compared to other world religions, Islam imposes a relatively more rigid commitment on its followers regular times for worship, physical sacrifice, etc. With its visible manifestations in public life, Islam's great discipline appears more rigorous. In a post-religious, secular environment, some symbols such as men sporting beards and women wearing the headscarf (*Arabic: Ḥijāb*) may seem rigid and Muslims may be seen as too 'obsessed' with their religion. Some even may feel threatened by this external religiosity, fearing that Muslims are not able to coexist with others in a secular setting.

Young Muslims have to navigate through their religious commitment and the scrutiny they face from society, with the "big brother" media always watching them. Although, for the majority of Muslims, such public religious manifestations are rooted in their spirituality or love of God, which gives them confidence in themselves, this may be a daunting prospect for some young Muslims and the cause of their insularity, just as it may be one fault line of friction with their parents.

It is in the nature of young people to rebel against established social norms and to have a passion to bring an immediate change in the world. This impatience, coupled with the vulnerability of young people in a permissive society, creates gaps between many of them and their parents who may feel a "loss of control" over their youngsters. Passive and inconsistent family disciplining of children in adolescence, or sometime enthusiastic draconian restrictions, can make things worse. Some parents give up and withdraw from their children's lives. If this is not handled properly at home and in the institutions of the community, schools cannot do much and young people can fall prey into the hands of online groomers of sex and extremism.

The parents' responsibility to deal effectively with their children is vital. This includes understanding their own children and the surrounding factors in an ever-changing social environment as well as educating and mentoring them until they grow into responsible adults. Mere clinging to an "Islamic duty" of advice or admonishment to fulfil ritual religious practices is not enough in these times. The children will be left neither here nor there if parents ignore their own responsibility or provide poor parenting and then blame society.

Parental love, care and quality time at home are the antidotes to cultural and generational gaps that may develop in families and then gradually affect the whole community. Some ordinary parents, with a humble background in education and an average earning, have no communication gap at all with their smart children who are always highly appreciative of them.

Young people's energy and creative thinking, when channelled properly, are an asset to any society. As the future leaders of their nations, they continuously need motivation to succeed. They need empathy, guidance, role modelling and a better engagement from the adults around them. Sadly, mental health is also one of the factors affecting sections of the Muslim youth. Depression, family problems, drugs and alcohol related stress, on the one hand, and prejudice, racism and Islamophobia, on the other, contribute in the development of mental illnesses. Some individuals are not diagnosed early and suffer in silence.

Young Muslims still love their mosques and have an affinity with them, even though some mosques exclude them while some youth have also been drifting away from religion in recent times. Small and resource-constrained mosques may not have the physical capacity to engage young people adequately, but where there is a will there is a way. Imams and people who manage the mosques should find better and creative ways of engaging with adolescents.

The synergy existing between families and their local mosques and institutions is vital in reducing cultural and generational gaps in the community. Getting children involved in local community institutions is itself a success, as it will help the community's regeneration and progress. Mosques should be hubs for the local people if they want to uplift the community through various activities like education, health provision, economic and social activities and interfaith. They can be the catalyst of inter-community harmony with the broader agenda of achieving the common good.

7

Consistency in using
Discipline Techniques

Disciplining children

Children are not small adults. They are newcomers to this world and everything is new to them. They view the world through fresh and curious eyes and minds. They are inquisitive, playful, imaginative and often impressionable. Even when they grow up into adolescents, they may still be uncritical and driven by idealistic or altruistic motivations. Their lives are about exploring and learning; they often live in a fantasy world and do not bother trying to make sense of what they see and hear in their early years. Their thinking is short-termed and often about their own needs. Children need to be informed about the world and what to do and what not to do. This is how they learn about obedience, authority and discipline. Adults around them should guide them and lovingly prepare them in their formative lives while granting them some freedom.

Discipline is about streamlining children's behaviour with positive guidance. It is also about reducing undesirable behaviours so that they are kept safe. It could be set in the form of instructions for children to follow particular codes of conduct. Children discipline is about setting simple, implementable rules, generally with rewards and penalties, to teach them self-discipline and desirable behaviours. Bite-size tasks that children are able to carry out enhance their self-esteem and confidence. This aims to develop in them basic human qualities and acceptable social habits that become embedded in their character. Self-disciplined children grow up into adults who have positive characters, sound judgements and good morals.

The issue of children's discipline is of major concern to parents, teachers and other professionals who deal with children. There are various perspectives regarding children's discipline, such as behavioural models, developmental psychology, social work and religious understanding. Human beings are multi-dimensional; and just as values, beliefs, education, customs and cultures vary, so too do the methods of children's discipline. The age, mental maturity and temperament of children are important factors.

Discipline is not tantamount to punishment, although punishment may be an important element of it. The corporal punishment of children was in the past customary in almost all societies, cultures and religious communities. It is strongly recommended in the Old Testament. The adage 'Spare the rod, spoil the child', although not a biblical quote, was applied religiously over the centuries. The Prophet of Islam (peace and blessings be upon him) approved applying a mild form of punishment on one's children, upon reaching the age of ten, if they fail to perform the compulsory prayer. But according to Muslim jurists, this should be the last resort and must be done without showing any harshness or anger.

Corporal punishment is still prevalent in many societies around the world. There has been an extensive debate in the recent past about the corporal punishment of children in western countries. In fact, the corporal punishment of children in some of these countries has all but disappeared. Attention now is increasingly given to the concept of 'positive parenting' at home and 'assertive discipline' in schools in which good behaviour is encouraged or rewarded and negative behaviour is somehow penalised.

Discipline is the bridge that links goals with accomplishments. As children grow, they learn from their parents and other adults close to them. The family, school, the neighbourhood and the wider society all contribute to children's journey of development. Children grow with informal and formal rules and regulations, or discipline techniques, that bind them. The period of human development is much longer than that of any other created being. A knowledge-based, progressive society is advantaged in its effective disciplining of children.

Positive discipline starts early in life, well before children start misbehaving. The family is the bedrock of human society and the parents behave as an anchor and role model for their children. Children tend to follow the behaviour and conduct of their parents and other adults and individuals around them.

Good schooling is vital in instilling good manners in children through positive discipline. Schools should focus on assertive discipline techniques so that children acquire self-discipline and respect for others as well as for the environment. A good school should have an agreed upon comprehensive behaviour policy with robust monitoring and implementation strategies rewards for good behaviour and penalties for any violation of this policy. Setting reasonably high standards of behaviour is important in helping children to feel safe, so that they can learn with love.

Positive disciplining techniques

Disciplining children is about helping and guiding them to grow up as responsible human beings possessing a positive behaviour and the ability to make good choices in life. In all cultures, children have a pivotal importance in the family and social life as a whole, as they are the future of their nations. Childhood innocence gives an immense joy to parents. Children are vulnerable, and so children's discipline has to be sensitive. 'Do not train a child to learn by force or harshness; but direct them to it by what amuses their minds, so that you may be better able to discover with accuracy the peculiar bent of the genius of each,'[22] said Greek philosopher and teacher Plato.

Children learn fast. Parents and carers should discipline their children only when this is needed at the right time when children do something out of order in order to correct their inappropriate behaviour. Robust, but rational and consistent discipline through simple incentives and sanctions is important for children's natural growth and motivation. Here are a few simple tips for the rational disciplining of children.

a) Treating children as children

Children should not be treated as adults and their innocence should be preserved at any cost, especially when they are unable to express themselves. As they go to school and get older, they become more able to talk about their feelings, understand and follow rules. Then they start developing self-control to deal with their frustrations and disappointments. Parental love, assurance and modelling are vital for children.

b) Involving children in setting boundaries and rules

Children may be tender in age but it is vital they are given the respect they deserve. Parents should explain their position, listen to their children's opinions and then compromise where and when needed. Children may come up with all sorts of excuses or examples to avoid doing certain things, and so, it is helpful to get them involved in discussions. Parents should not be too stubborn about things they can be flexible about; they

---

22 https://www.goodreads.com/

should not allow their egos to dictate their decisions or fear losing face when dealing with their young ones.

c) Parents must be gentle but firm

Parents must let their children know that it is safe to express their feelings respectfully. If children act strangely with their parents, then it should be remembered that everyone has his or her bad days they should be told to speak nicely. When they calm down, the parents should talk gently with them about what was making them unhappy. Respect goes both ways, so parents should speak with their children the way they wish them to speak with them. Parents should not tell their children off or raise their voices in a way that may seem like shouting. Parents should say what they want to say in a clear and calm manner. Moreover, they should not forget to say "please" and "thank you."

d) Using do's and don'ts with measure

Human life should not be regimented, as in the military, and structured around command and obedience. Life is not black and white. Parents should focus on the behaviour they want to see in their children and not on what they are doing wrong. Fault-finding often destroys relationships. Instead of being angry or shouting: 'Don't throw that ball or pen', parents should instead say: 'throwing the ball or pen could hurt someone or break something.' On occasions, parents can distract their children from misbehaving by saying: 'Let's go outside or let's do something.'

e) Finding out what lies behind children's behaviour

Human beings are complex. Even though children are less complex than adults, there are reasons for their misbehaviour and disobedience such as environmental and psychological factors that parents may not know.

Maybe one's son was rude to a playmate because he had had too many activities that day; or maybe one's daughter was abrasive to one because someone had poked fun at her in school. Parents should step back and consider the reasons that cause their children to misbehave. Later, when they calm down, they should be asked about what happened to them.

f) Keeping discipline simple

One's school-going child may be better able to understand rules, but one should avoid going into too much details. A lemon gets bitter if one squeezes it too hard. Over-enthusiasm in following rules or asking for explanations about small things could be counter-productive. If soft power works in a situation, parents should never use hard power. Children go through phases. While parents should keep an eye on their children, they should only deal with misbehaviour when needed.

g) Being consistent regarding family rules

Children should be involved in and consulted about family rules so that they are clear about what to do and what to avoid. When parents waver or become inconsistent about family rules, children will realise that they can push the boundaries further the next time. Inconsistency conveys to the children the negative message that parents are not certain about what they are asking of them. So parents should consult their children, establish simple family rules and enforce them effectively and with love.

h) Avoiding hard-hitting discipline measures

Whatever children's misbehaviour is and regardless of its cause, parents should avoid shouting and angry exchanges with their children. Ultimately, parents are the leaders of their family. They should never use violence in any situation, however hurt they may feel. Parents' outbursts are demeaning and undermine their authority in the eyes of their children. A parent who struggles with controlling his or her anger should learn anger management.

i) Turning negatives into positives

Anger is a fire that can burn relationships, but controlled anger is important to tackle children's rude behaviour or aggression. Negative features or emotions are embedded in human nature and one has the power to turn them into positive features and emotions. Just as controlled fire is needed for some useful things, such as cooking, controlled anger also is essential for fighting against injustice and oppression. Successful parents are able to turn their children's negative behaviours into positive outcomes through patience and ingenuity. Negative behaviours simply require more thoughtfulness and wisdom.

8

Helping one's children to find true friends

Each baby is born from a father and a mother: bare and dependent on them as well as on other adults for its survival. One's departure from the world is also a lonely journey. Life is a mystery. Death is the abiding reality that will one day visit every person. Between birth and death, one lives a life of tests and trials according to Islam. In this transitory world, people are inter-linked and inter-dependent. One has no control over one's birth or death. Each person works for his or her own destiny.

Children rely on their parents and carers while the elderly and weak rely on their children or other people. People need certain people more than others – parents, children, spouses, close family members, friends, professionals, etc. Apart from one's blood-related members and relatives, one's friends play a vital role in one's life.

Children in current times are massively influenced by their peers, electronic gadgets (particularly mobiles) and role models. In the world of "compulsive consumerism", children are surrounded by the newest models of attractive gadgets through ads in electronic and print media; the promotion of celebrity role models is no less invasive considering their impressionable minds. However, children can choose to make friends with whoever they want. Friendship is crucial in children's lives and can be more powerful than their relationship with their parents and siblings. True and trusted friends are a blessing, as they selflessly help and provide strong emotional support in life.

Everyone needs good friends and companions. The ancient proverbs: 'We can live without a brother, but not without a friend' and 'A life without a friend is a life without a sun' are illuminating. A friendship with someone who is trustworthy, both inwardly and outwardly, can help one's spirituality.

> **You will not find anyone who believes in Allah and the Last Day, making friendship with those who oppose Allah and His Messenger, even though they were their fathers, sons, brothers or their relatives.**
> (Qur'an, 58:22)

Prophet Muhammad (peace and blessings be upon him) gave a clear message regarding friendship: 'A person follows the faith of his bosom friend, so let one of you consider who he befriends.' (Abū Dawūd and al-Tirmidhī)

Children choose their friendships from their surroundings in school and neighbourhood, and caring parents can assist them in that. Some friendships struck by children in their early age remain for the rest of their lives. Other friends join in as they grow, as sociability and real life situations, such as their job and proximity, help in finding new friends. From the Islamic point of view, the question one should keep in mind is whether such friendships are based on trust and even useful on not in the Day of Judgement.

> And (remember) the Day when the wrong-doer will bite his hands and say: Woe to me! Would that I had taken a path with the Messenger. Woe to me! If only I had not taken so and so as a friend! He has led me astray from this Reminder (the Qur'an) after it had come to me. And Satan is ever a deserter to man in the hour of need.
> (Qur'an, 25:27-29)

> Friends on that Day will be enemies one to another, except the righteous.
> (Qur'an, 43:67)

Prophet Muhammad (peace and blessings be upon him) used a metaphor to distinguish good friends from bad friends:

> *The example of a good companion and a bad companion is like the example of the seller of musk and the one who blows the blacksmith's bellows. The seller of musk either gives you some musk, you buy some from him, or at least you enjoy a pleasant smell from him. As for the one who blows the blacksmith's bellows, he either burns your clothes or you will get an offensive smell from him.*
> (Bukhārī and Muslim)

The Prophet advised his followers to 'mix with noble people and you become one of them; and keep away from evil people to protect yourself from their evils.' (Bukhārī and Muslim)

The best example of friendship is that between the Prophet Muhammad (peace and blessings be upon him) and his most trusted friend and Companion Abū Bakr (may Allah be pleased with him). During his migration (*Arabic: Hijrah*) from Makkah to Madinah, Abū

Bakr was chosen as the Prophet's co-traveller in their long journey. Abū Bakr sacrificed everything for the sake of God and the service of the Prophet.

Choosing true friends

Most young people nowadays have a large number of friends, some in school or youth clubs, but mostly through the social media such as Facebook and other online platforms. The question is: how many of these friends do they know personally and how well? Moreover, of the friends that one knows, how many are those who would pass the test of being "a friend in need is a friend indeed"? Online friends, some artificial or false, constitute a real concern for parents as discussed in Chapter 14. The golden rule is that, while children may have as many normal friends as they can manage, the common wisdom is that they should have a small number of true and trusted friends.

Choosing a friend sounds very simple and sociable children are better than others in making friends. However, finding true friends needs some intuition and a simple method of testing. An ancient proverb says: 'Prove a friend before you seek him.' It may not be that easy for young children to be selective, as they tend to hang around and make friends with anyone they can easily get along with. Parents and guardians should guide their children to choose true friends through taking a loving, but not intrusive, interest in their lives.

Being friends to all human beings is vital. A Muslim should be a good friend to others as well as to nature. However, a true friend is chosen on the basis of one's faith, practice, trustworthiness and other good human traits. According to a saying of Prophet Muhammad (peace and blessings be upon him), 'The believer is the mirror of other believers.' True friends from a believing community would always give an honest and straightforward advice to their friends; they forgive mistakes, but they do not hide or exaggerate the strengths and weaknesses of their true friends.

Once the Prophet was asked, 'Who is the best friend?' He answered, 'He who helps you remember Allah and reminds you when you forget Him.' Such a friend reflects the qualities taught by Islam such as love, honesty, patience, optimism, professionalism, etc. Wise Muslim sages of the past left to posterity some gems regarding true friends. Here are some of them: 'Do not befriend a fool for he will harm you whence he means to do you good' ; 'it is better to listen to a wise enemy than to seek counsel from a foolish friend'; 'if a friend envies you, then he is not a true friend'.

Islam's fourth Caliph Alī (may Allah be pleased with him) said, 'Verily, the Muslim has three (types of) friends: (1) a friend who says: "I am with you whether you are alive or dead," this is his deeds; (2) a friend who says: "I am with you up to the threshold of your grave and then I will leave you," this is his children; (3) and a friend who says: "I will be with you until you die," this is his wealth which will go to his inheritors upon his death.'

For people of faith, friendship based on belief and God-consciousness is the only true and lasting friendship. On the other hand, friendship based on materialistic and selfish motives is transient and detrimental to one's Hereafter. A good friend is someone whose company brings blessings, increases knowledge and enhances spirituality. True friendship inspires one's devotion to Allah and His Prophet (peace and blessings be upon him) as well as loyalty to one's parents and family, as they are aware that their own children would inherit their qualities.

The features of the true friend

Friendship made at young age usually last longer, but as children grow older, they also make new friends. Losing a friend can be sometimes heart-breaking, especially when a friendship has been longstanding. However, it is important to acknowledge that not all friendships last. With time and experience and the help of parents, children learn better how to choose reliable and true friends.

True friendship is about reciprocating good manners and advice and being mutual role models. It is about overlooking the small mistakes of one's friends without abdicating the duty of reminding each other of goodness. True friendship spreads cheerfulness, summons good conversation and speech and encourages largeness of the soul. It spreads inward qualities such as inner purity, external modesty and overall cleanliness. Agreement with friends on everything is not a condition; dignified disagreement may be necessary. True friends are happy with each other's success; God censures those who are envious: 'Or do they envy men for what Allah has given them from His bounty' (Qur'an, 4:94). The Prophet said: 'Do not envy one another.' (*Ṣaḥīḥ* Muslim)

The following are some of the characteristics of true friends according to the Islamic teachings:

- They always meet each other, or start their conversation, with reciprocated greetings of peace and leave each other's company with a higher level of faith.
- They listen to each other and exchange useful, positive and mature ideas and thoughts.
- They do not hesitate to correct each other's mistakes or bad habits, and they do this with humility
- They do not waste each other's time in vain talk or useless activities.
- They never encourage one another to do wrong things, nor do they invite each other to places of obscenity.
- They stand firm regarding the truth when required.
- They wish good for one another and ask for God's guidance.

One should be mature and wise enough to know who one's true friends are. At the same time, it is vital that one knows the characteristics of fake friends in order to keep away from them; here are some of the characteristics of fake friends:

- They avoid compulsory acts of worship or they are not serious about them.
- They backbite and make fun of people using demeaning names or cruel jokes.
- They discuss idle issues and entice others to gratify their greed and sensual desires. They are not serious about earning a lawful living or spending their money on lawful things just as they are bent on extravaganzas.
- They accommodate others' mistakes and wrongs.
- They are proven to be 'fair weather friends.'

9

Tackling teenage issues sensitively

The onset of adolescence during which a child grows into an adult brings huge energy and some flair to the young person undergoing it. Adolescence, which is also described as the teenage years between 13 and 19 during which the biological changes of puberty take place, often brings some anxiety and challenges to parents and other adults in the family. This period of change in children brings similar hopes and concerns in all cultures, communities and nations; and this is more so for immigrant and newly settled communities.

'Little children, headache; big children, heartache', says an Italian Proverb. There may be an ancient wisdom in this, as handling teenage children may be dreadful for some parents. But the good news is that most families fair generally well through the challenges of this phase in their children's growth. Enjoyment and excitement are also to be found in children's age of puberty when parents are aware of what is coming and prepare themselves with some techniques and strategies. In the long run, many parents find this 'headache and heartache' more fulfilling.

Adolescents can be the source of comfort or nightmares. They generally provoke criticism from elders for their restlessness and often rash and impulsive outbursts. On the other hand, they symbolise a new life with dreams, vision, creative enterprise, vitality and enthusiasm. Adolescence is a phase in life when children discover their energy and potential to aspire for things that are often unusual, audacious and exploratory. If driven by a positive, moral and spiritual ethos in life, as was the case with many teenage Prophetic Companions (*Ṣaḥāba* in Arabic, sing: *Ṣaḥābī*) during the blessed time of Prophet Muhammad (peace and blessings be upon him), the community could lift itself to great heights. On the other hand, the misdirected energy of adolescence can destroy individuals and create havoc in society.

The story of Britain's adolescents in recent times is mixed, and not always encouraging. A World Health Organisation (WHO) study in 2016 found that Britain's teenagers[23] are stressed, drink too much and think they are fat; they are also the 'least satisfied in the western world'. There is also an imbalance in the press coverage of young people. On the other hand, due the security focus on the Muslim community, the higher proportion of young Muslims in prison and ISIS recruits since 2014, it is difficult to get an accurate picture on Muslim teenagers. However, it is recognised that some of them suffer from mental health problems while others are more affected by inner city issues.

Children generally mirror what their parents give them in their early years. They also learn from their surroundings – neighbourhoods, schools, communities or youth centres. As they reach adolescence and begin their exciting journey into adulthood, they undergo astonishing changes in their bodies, feelings and thought processes. Growing up is

---

23 http://www.independent.co.uk/news/uk/home-news/britain-s-teenagers-are-stressed-drink-too-much-and-think-they-re-fat-a6932431.html

a once-in-a-lifetime, complex experience which is exhilarating for some and challenging for others. Adolescence is a period of inner commotion and struggle for young people. The changes that they undergo are physical, emotional, social, intellectual and spiritual, each of which is a test for them.

The physical change, known as puberty, activates their bodies' clock to function in a different mode which prepares them to be physically capable of reproduction. This is reflected by the production of increasing amounts of oestrogen in girls, and testosterone in boys that turn them into women and men respectively; this change in bodily hormones is a totally new experience for them and creates in them an immense attraction to the opposite sex. Adolescents may be driven to lose their innocence with unethical boy-girl relationships if the environment is indulgent; young practising Muslim boys and girls who believe that sexual relationship is permissible only within marriage try to build their inner spiritual resilience and avoid illicit relationships.

The physical growth of adolescents itself causes them some embarrassment. As they do not have any control over their physical growth, this naturally imposed change may create feelings of confusion in them. The ensuing psychological and emotional changes can make them unreasonable and unpredictable and they may be perceived differently by people around them. Adolescents know that they are still dependant on their parents, but they are aware that they must become self-reliant and more independent. They try to assert themselves and often do this in ways that may seem unreasonable and disruptive to their household routines. Some adolescents tend to push the boundaries that their parents might have previously set. For example, they may resent participating in family activities or be discourteous to younger siblings or even be rude to elders. They may be interested in reading adult books or magazines, listening to loud music, watching more TV programmes and spending more time with smartphones which their parents may not like. They may style themselves with weird hair styles and fashion, come home late and refuse to go shopping with their parents or participate in family-orientated activities. They may nag their parents to buy them certain expensive designer clothes, games or electronic gadgets.

Many adolescents are greatly influenced by their friends and the role models they encounter in the electronic, print and social media. Adolescence is a period when some may suffer from insecurity, eating disorders, egocentrism or mental health issues. This could make them rude to their parents, teachers and other adults, and even rebellious. It is at this stage that parents need to show their utmost love, patience and empathy with their adolescent children. Parents must adapt with this situation and change their own attitudes and habits towards their children positively; they should consider their adolescents as individuals in their own right. The parenting skills and styles employed in raising them in the early stages should be adapted to accommodate their adolescent children.

As children reach puberty, their parents should be able to discuss sensitively with them the onset of adulthood, career and the rights and duties of adult life. A healthy and loving parent-child relationship is essential for good discussions about life issues. Sensitive parents do not put too much pressure on their adolescent children to fit in the adult world. Rather, they give them space and time to settle on their own. On the other hand, they cannot afford to be too libertarian or neglectful; they must not abdicate their basic parental duties. Children are under enormous pressure to conform to the youth culture of the day. The best strategy in this phase is adopting a positive, rational and flexible attitude, one which is polite but assertive. Parents need to keep in mind that, although they are not their children's friends, they should be friendly with them. Most children appreciate this 'tough love' approach from parents and teachers. Adolescents should never feel they are ignored or under-valued nor should they feel that they can get away with any unacceptable behaviour.

One of the most effective strategies for parents at this period in their children's lives is to remain consistent in their behaviour and empathetic with their adolescent children who should be given enough natural praise, space, appreciation and respect. Adolescents should be involved in family affairs and household chores as well as in neighbourhood and community life. They should be given the opportunity to enjoy their lives, albeit in a wholesome way. Parents should avoid angry exchanges with their adolescent children or stupidly quarrelling with one another; parental discord can be too much to bear for adolescents, which may drive them to look for a better life outside of their homes. A consistent family routine which is agreed upon in the family through consultation such as family time, eating together, etc. is helpful. A home should be a place of solace for all family members.

Parents should watch out and keep an extra eye on what happens in their children's schools during the period of their adolescence. Parents should constantly ask themselves the following questions: Is there any sign of unhappiness brought from school or from outside home due to, say, bullying or discrimination? Is something bothering them? Who are their best friends? Are there gangsters, drugs, violence or extremism in their vicinity or local community that may tempt their adolescent children?

Then there are the vital questions of motivation and aspiration in this period of adolescence. Are their adolescent children doing well educationally as well as individuals? Do they have enough self-esteem and confidence with their inclusive identity? Are they happy with themselves and self driven? Do they show interest in their family, neighbourhood and community affairs? Parents using simple observation and insight are able to 'read' their adolescent children's minds by looking at their face and noticing their behaviour and body language. Any early sign of difficulty can then be addressed with sensitivity.

In a world of indulgence and crave for self-gratification, growing as a self-respecting and self-motivated human being with a community ethos and shared social values is a huge challenge for most young people. Teenagers will have ups and downs in this phase of their growth and may go through mood swings and erratic behaviour. They may even be at the threshold of a very turbulent life. A balanced view of life may not be within reach for many of them. It may also be challenging to some adolescents to understand the world around them and carve out a role in it. Parents and the adults around teenagers should be available to listen to and advise them; for they need unconditional love and affection from parents as well as a wholesome environment.

Young people are inherently innocent, instinctively happy and energetic; they bring a fresh perspective to elders and their company transmits liveliness and innocence. Fortunate is the community or nation that succeeds in harnessing the potentials of its teenagers and prepares them for its future leadership.

10

Instilling family values in one's children

Young people and Social trend

Marriage and the family have been two sacred core institutions since the dawn of humanity. From time immemorial, the family constituted through the marriage of a man and a woman has been the most fundamental social organisation. There have been highs and lows in human history regarding these two institutions, but they have continued to survive and keep providing love, care, compassion and other indispensable values in different societies, nations and the world at large.

However, as a result of massive changes in attitude vis-à-vis life since the Industrial Revolution, and with the advent of new lifestyles and social trends, the institution of marriage has weakened. Since World War II, marriage has lost much of its relevance in western developed countries and, as a result, the family structure has been changing, giving rise to blended families[24] (some call it step families), where one or both parents have children from a previous relationship. Women's changed economic status , the liberalisation of divorce laws, the legalisation of abortion, the availability of contraceptives and social acceptance of 'love children' have all been contributing factors in this change.

With the emergence of non-traditional gender roles in modern times, men and women are often seen as competitors rather than complementing each other[25] as mentioned in the Qur'an. The unprecedented rise in individualism is also having its effect and there is nowadays a tendency in people to expect receiving more than they are ready to give themselves. Such an attitude affects marriage which is a long term commitment. Moreover, some young adults in marriageable age are not well equipped with the necessary emotional and intellectual maturity, compassion and patience required in marriage. Marital problems and predicaments in developed societies have rocketed in recent decades, giving rise to domestic violence and child abuse. This is spreading into many social groups, including the burgeoning Muslim communities of western countries.

In recent decades, like in the wider society, Muslim men and women have been getting married late in life. There appears to be a lack of seriousness concerning marriage among young Muslim men and women or, else, prospective spouses make too rigid demands before they get married. Divorce rates are also getting higher, even among practising Muslims. This is a matter of great concern and worry in the Muslim community. As the wider society is increasingly shunning religion, under the influence of its consumerist and entertainment culture, one also detects some decline in religious attachment in some sections of

---

24 See, Stepfamilies Are Becoming The Norm, So Let's Retire Cinderella: How Stepfamilies Can Learn To Thrive, by Glen-Peter Ahlers Sr. – Child and Family Law Journal, Vol4, Issue 1, 2016; and http://family.lovetoknow.com/definition-blended-family

25 Qur'an, 78:8.

the Muslim community. This is having an adverse impact on parents' attempt to instil family values in their children.

Equipping children with family values

First generation Muslim parents, especially those coming from rural backgrounds in the developing world, are obviously at a disadvantage in effectively raising their children in the complex social realities of life in western developed countries. Some do struggle, particularly in handling their children's teenage period. The relatively wide cultural gap between first generation parents and their young children, who have grown up in fast-paced technological societies, is an additional challenge for these parents. Nowadays young people spend nowadays more time online with different social media which leaves them little time to interact with their parents.

The lives of young people nowadays are significantly different from the lives of their parents' generation. In a socially liberal world, children's rights are often put above the rights of parents, which sometimes confuses these parents. The early loss of childhood innocence due to the over-sexualisation of society is also having its toll, in terms of premature sex and its negative outcomes such as teenage pregnancy and educational under-achievement.

Parenting for religious people is about preparing the future generation to succeed in life, both in this world and the hereafter. As this is heavily affected by external factors in modern times; parents have to bear in mind that they have a continuous and constant task to turn their little angels into good human beings in just ten to fifteen years. Preparing youngsters with a moral ethos in life and universal human values is a monumental task indeed.

Raising children with family values from an early age is vital in a pluralist society. Home, as the bastion of primary educational training for young people, should crucially prepare them with these values before they enter the world as adults. Social values, such as tolerance, respect and civic organising for social justice, are vital for individuals in any civilised society; political values, such as treating all equally, respecting diversity and agreeing to disagree, are essential for living peacefully as citizens; religious values, such as empathy, compassion and modesty, are matters that enrich people's hearts.[26]

Similarly, work related values, such as the ability to work in a team or treating colleagues at work with dignity, improves the culture and outcome of organisation. Moral values, such as patience, trustworthiness and personal responsibility, provide a strong foundation for any society. Recreational values, such as spending time together and having an opportunity to relax and learn, foster closeness in the family.

However, for Muslim children to grow up soundly in a pluralist secular society, parents have to enhance their confidence in their ethnic and cultural roots. A home environment where the relationship between the parents is based on love, compassion and respect is naturally a pulling factor for children. On the other hand, a family riven by heated arguments or domestic violence may push children away. Children who grow up in a spiritually rich family environment stand at an advantage with regard to personal humility, empathy and respect in their relationship with the people around them.

There has to be a positive and lively interaction with young people in daily life along with regular one-to-one quality time with each child as they start school. Parents must also create a sense of family bonding through various ways, such as shopping or visiting interesting places together, frequent eating together and regular family sessions. Continuous natural encouragement of children's positive behaviour and action as well as watching and listening approvingly to them make them feel valued and help to shape their self-image. Children may come up with endless curious queries and questions and the parents' encouragement and patience, without criticism, enhance their relationship. Children's exposure to their nearest role models –

---

26 See, *Family Values: The Ethics of Parent-Child Relationships*, by Harry Brighouse and Adam Swift, Princeton University Press, 2014.

their mums and dads at home – is obviously the most effective way of teaching them family values.

During family events at home, depending on the level of maturity, older children may be invited to help or even take a lead in these activities. When specific topics of family values, or any other contemporary issues, are discussed, children may be asked to give their opinion. If done effectively, this will enhance the ethos of consultation in children and improve their confidence. Children may be given the task of listing ideas on behalf of their parents which can then be prioritised to a manageable number of around five tasks and displayed in a prominent place. Home is not only where family members live but also a teaching institution for them.

11

Core duties and basic rights in the family

A very learned, wise and successful Asian father that I know sent me an email a while ago in which he wrote: 'The motto of a budding family should be parenting, parenting, parenting. Many problems caused by adolescents could be avoided through proper parental care and discipline. A large share of the blame for the 2011 summer riot in England is on the parents who are not doing their job properly.'

This resonates with social reality on responsible parenting, although the situation is slightly more complex in today's rights-based society. A society based on a robust family structure, in which parental authority is used lovingly and effectively, will more likely transform the energy of its youths into nation building elements. And wherever the family structure is weak, the energy of the youths turn into the kind of disorder one sees in the inner city streets of many developed countries.

The family is the core organisation of any society. Effective, positive and assertive parenting should be at the heart of every family in order for society to advance. Children grow under the care of adults, fully dependent on them for their survival, protection and development. The mother and father are naturally the first people in a child's life. Not only do they make sure of their children's balanced growth but they also preserve and strengthen their family's intellectual, cultural and spiritual heritage.

In a powerful speech at the Labour Party Conference in 1996, the labour leader who became Britain's Prime Minister, Tony Blair, set the tone of his future government: 'Ask me my three main priorities for Government, and I tell you: education, education and education.' Education is vital for any country's progress. The Meiji rulers in Japan transformed their country in the 1870s and 1880s through their bold and innovative educational plan.

However, education starts at home with good-quality parenting. 'Home is the best school' goes the old maxim.

Parenting means more than the mere raising of children. It is a conscious endeavour that starts from the moment a baby is conceived in its mother's womb. It is the duty of parents to give such a conscious attention to their baby in its embryonic stage; it is also a basic right of every baby to be nourished and nurtured by its parent.

The task of parenting does not end with children's puberty or when they reach the age of sixteen or eighteen. In the Islamic tradition, it continues until one's offspring reach the age of twenty-one. In fact, it is a life-long commitment that involves the physical, intellectual, emotional, social and spiritual wellbeing of the child beginning from its conception in the womb. Of course, the nature of parenting changes as children grow from dependence to inter-dependence in their adult lives.

The reward of effective parenting is enormous and long-lasting. On the other hand, poor parenting or abdicating parental responsibility can bring distressing consequences for the family, wider society and the nation as a whole.

Parenting is essentially about preparing children for the future, a one-time opportunity to set them on the right path for life. The historic adage, 'the hand that rocks the cradle, rules the world', is remembered and wisely practised by successful nations.

The primary ingredient of parenting is love. However, as children grow, 'blind love' should be gradually replaced by 'tough love'; the tough love of raising children with consistent and rational boundaries, educating them and instilling in them good manners. Children obviously need the opportunity and freedom to naturally grow as 'good human beings'. Discipline is vital in one's life, and it is far more so for children during their adolescence..

Parenting is about motivating children to think positively and act constructively. This could be an uphill task in communities or groups that suffer from socio-economic disadvantages and the onslaught of negative media portrayals and social stigma. The challenges facing Muslims have multiplied after the 7/7 London bombings, the murder of Lee Rigby in 2013 and the emergence of Daesh (ISIS) in 2014 in the Middle East. The natural tendency of some people, who are 'cornered' by the media and political establishments, is to withdraw from society. Creating ghettoized communities is tantamount to defeatism and is counter-productive for the future of nations. It also leads to the polarisation of the whole society. Young people are real assets and the future leaders of any society; no developed democratic society should be allowed to squander its human resources.

Muslim parents, a significant number of whom are still first generation immigrants, put educational achievement at the heart of their parenting duties. However there is still a high level of social deprivation in the Muslim community as well as external disadvantages. The 2016 report of Social Mobility Commission, *Ethnicity, Gender and Social Mobility* [27] highlighted the 'broken promises for many groups' in Britain that are struggling for good jobs and better opportunities in

---

27 https://www.gov.uk/government/uploads/system/uploads/attachment_data/
file/579988/Ethnicity_gender_and_social_mobility.pdf

life. One of these groups is the Asian Muslims, and more particularly Muslim Asian women. According to this report, although children of Pakistani and Bangladeshi origins, especially girls, are doing better than average in educational achievements, this is not translated into a change for them in the labour market. Higher unemployment rates among them have thwarted their overall economic progress and keep holding back their social mobility. Only a small number of people within this group have managerial or professional occupations.

Although there is no magic wand to solve all these issues, there are ways of moving up the socio-economic ladder in a meritocratic society like Britain. Parents, the community and other institutions, like religious or youth centres, have a wider role to play in improving children's education and job prospects through entrepreneurial initiatives. The community is over-represented in some professions, such as medicine and accountancy, and it is high time that other social and human sciences are given the same importance.

In post-9/11 which abounds with a disproportionate, and often unfair, anti-Muslim media focus on young Muslims particularly, the parents' role in helping their children to face prejudice, bigotry and bullying in schools and the streets is vital. Parents must also consider their children's vulnerability towards delinquency, drugs and extremism which are a reality in some parts of Britain's inner cities.

There is now more demand for a movement of grass-root parenting in the community, with individual parents getting seriously involved in teaching their children relevant skills and investing in their future and that of their country. Mosque and community institutions can remind and even take initiative in running parenting courses. They can also facilitate adult education and English language courses for those who need them.

Confident parents are able to create a positive home environment and impart in their children, especially in their adolescence, the self-esteem and drive needed to succeed in life. Parents and community activists should work with their local schools, faith institutions and local governments to collectively address these issues so that the younger generations develop a sense of worth as citizens.

Of course, parenting transcends mere duties and rights in the family; it also transcends mechanical and legalistic rituals. Parenting is more than the mere carrying out of the basic task of looking after one's children at home, as no family can raise its children in isolation. Parenting is about building neighbourhoods, communities, societies and nations. It is about giving children an inclusive vision of life and preparing them to work for the good of all and building a nation. It is about creating good citizens and, above all, good human beings.

12

Building an understanding of give-and-take

By Divine will, and through their union to form their own families, women and men jointly bring new lives to this world. As the building block of society, not only does the family nurture children, it also teaches and guides them to develop into good human beings. The family is built on the basis of shared responsibility amongst its members. The mother and father, as primordial leaders, complement one another and endeavour to create a future generation based on an understanding of give-and-take. Grounding this understanding well in children at home gives society an invaluable gift, that of giving preference to others.

A strong, stable and loving family environment produces confident and competent children with a positive outlook on life. When children grow with unlimited love in their early phases of development, as well as with moral and spiritual nurturing during their pre-adolescence period, this gives them an empathetic and positive attitude towards others; the impact that childhood education and training has on adult life is immense.

Parenting is a colossal responsibility. Raising children to grow as successful human beings is a noble task as well as a serious business. The mother's share of this responsibility that starts with pregnancy is exceedingly greater. As such, all cultures and religions have given mothers the highest respect. Both the mother and father have mutual rights and responsibilities in the family. Achieving a balance between these rights and responsibilities needs some noble qualities such as honesty, tolerance, justice, compassion and warmth. Parents should also shy away from some negative traits such as arrogance, haughtiness, pessimism, impatience and selfishness. All this needs continuous soul-searching and a determined action to stay on the middle way of life.

In any family, the woman, as wife, and the man, as husband, take charge of their offspring and are obligated to give them everything they need in life. Both of them often put their personal differences aside and give their best in the raising of their children; together they make the family a happy union and act as force of good in society. The home has always been children's first school where they get a grip on their lives before facing the harsh realities of the world.

Raising children consciously and passing on positive family and social values to them is vital. One's life is a one-way traffic; no sensible individual would gamble with life and no parent should do so with their children's future.

For people of faith, parenting is not only about children's growth to maturity and educational achievement to succeed in this world, it is also about preparing them to succeed in the life to come[28] by practising their religious teachings. That is why in many religious traditions, such as

---

28 Our Lord! Give unto us in the world that which is good and in the Hereafter that which is good - (Qur'an, 2:201).

Islam, children are a test[29] as well as a trust and raising them properly is a religious obligation. Families must pass such a test and look well after the trust with which they have been entrusted.

One's journey in life is short and full of trials, tribulations and imperfections, but it is also about determination and struggle for what is better as stewardship on earth. One may start one's life as an idealist in adolescence only for this to be superseded by realism in adulthood as one comes to terms with life experiences which oscillate between hope and concern. Some people may become worn-out due to the constraints they face, and they may even fall into the whirlwind of mid-life crisis and experience anxiety and depression. But human resilience most often wins and people usually pick themselves up with the help of real-life know-how and wisdom to move forward.

All people are endowed with a reservoir of positive human qualities. It is up to them, as parents, to make sacrifices to build their families, neighbourhoods and societies with boundless love, care and respect which are essential for children, especially in their early years to their mid-teen period.

Compromise, but do not compromise ...

The similarities existing between people that make them human, and the differences that make them diverse, are a wondrous and miraculous sign on this earth. Life is multi-faceted and multi-coloured; people's diversified natures make their lives enjoyable, challenging and often testing. All people have their individual needs and ambitions, as well as egos; they also have their group needs and interests as families, communities and societies. People's own feelings and instincts are very important to them.

But what do people do when their whims and desires clash? Can they afford to stubbornly hold on to their own whims and desires without any regard to others? It can be disastrous if this happens between

---

29 Your wealth and your children are only a trial - (Qur'an, 64:15)

members of the same family; most families break up due to the absence of this basic understanding and practice of give-and-take, or the art of compromise between couples or family members.

The culture of compromise, or finding a middle ground, must the common ground of any two people who unite to form a family. The family starts with two individual 'I's that become a single 'we'. This is vital upon the start of raising their children; parents cannot afford to give mixed or inconsistent signals to their children. Synergy between both parents is the key to raising self-assured and unconfused children.

This does not mean that family life should never witness any disagreements, arguments or squabbles. Real life is full of challenges and family rows are inevitable. It is also a fact that compromising one's principles is sometimes not possible. Once a couple is blessed with children, the lack of compromise may happen regarding small issues such as household chores and day-to-day activities as well as major ones relating to earning and career. In situations such as these, the challenge lies in how the couple deals with differences in a thoughtful, civilised and humane manner.

In a family in which the relationship between the husband and wife is based on love, compassion, respect and empathy, all these differences are resolved through 'share and care' and reliance[30] (*Arabic: Tawakkul*) on God, as it is well-known that the fruit of reliance on God is contentment with His decree. With compromise becoming second nature, their relationship may be solidified even further. A pragmatic couple, with positive attitudes towards life, nurtures warmth, affection and understanding; they are able to use the art of compromise to navigate through any potential turbulence in their relationship. In fact, over time, most couples become acutely sensitive to each other's likes and dislikes. They learn how to avoid conflict while making decisions, whether small or big. 'Sacrifice for the sake of the children' is obviously one of the best decisions.

---

30 And whoever relies upon Allah – He will be sufficient for him – (Qur'an: 65:3)

The human mind is very complex and people's feelings are disparate. While conversing with one's spouse on potentially sensitive issues, one should always take a step back and think seriously about what one wants to achieve and how really important the issue at stake is? Is it worth arguing about? On a scale of, say, 1 to 10, where does one place the success rate of any particular discussion? Once one reaches a personal and positive response, one should try to make one's case in a nice and dignified manner. One should make sure one listens to one's spouse attentively; proper listening is a sign of respect as well as a good remedy for any family or social ills. One should think and approach the issue at stake with empathy, 'putting one's feet in one's spouse's shoes', and then negotiate with no trick and no hidden agenda. There is only a win-win situation in the family; the alternative is a loss for everyone.

There are simpler and better ways of handling compromise in the family – through the art of persuasion, negotiation or through a positive, but pro-active, dealing with one's partner, without any complexity, ill-feeling or aggression. No spouse should walk on a tightrope or become over-sensitive towards his or her spouse. One should come forth with honesty and discuss any issues with an open mind. Openness and transparency are essential in family life.

Continuous quality time with one's spouse, mutual love and respect, one-to-one relaxed chats, eating or going out together, exchanging gifts and occasional open discussions, or family sessions, enhance the spouses' understanding of each other and deepen their relationships. Women and men are equal in the eyes of God, but they are not the same physically and emotionally; and having a basic understanding of these similarities and differences is vital for both spouses.

Children are the future and their success is what parents endeavour to achieve. All parents want their children to be more successful in life – as human beings and citizens of their country. However, with the changing nature of modern societies, many parents are genuinely worried. Through investing in their children's future and with an understanding of give-and-take in the family, parents can realise their dreams.

13

Looking after the elderly and showing them respect and compassion

One's arrival in this world, physical survival in the early years and growth to maturity are dependent on the adults around one. our life, until death, is inter-dependent and inter-linked. In this one-way journey of life, one's parents and the people close to one are essential in shaping one.

Dependence and interdependence are the essence of human continuity. Nowhere is this clearer than in the family which is society's core institution. A secured family whose members are strongly bonded by love, affection and respect is an invaluable ingredient of any stable society. Dependence and interdependence in the family start with looking after the physical and other basic needs of children after their birth, and are also witnessed through the mutual dependence of generations and then looking after the elderly members of the family. This is a natural life cycle.

The community, society and state also have their roles to play, but upholding this humane ethos of care and support is the family's duty from 'the cradle to the grave,' so to speak.

The new parent syndrome

Months of fantasising about one's baby, the parents' strange dreams and worrisome thoughts come to an end when they hold their newborn baby in their arms. Tiny and fragile, it fills their lives with matchless happiness and a sense of responsibility as they are overwhelmed with the thought that their lives will never be the same again. The excitement, ecstasy and natural worry of being a parent can only be understood by those who have had children. A baby's journey in life starts with absolute vulnerability and mostly ends with frailty in old age.

All people want to be the best parents possible; their awareness of their babies' dependency and their desire to be good parents generate a great deal of energy as well as stress. A father discovers new, deeper feelings towards his wife. He observes with wonder her courage, strength and endurance during labour and cannot fail to admire her. A mother bears physical pain and emotional stress while waiting to see her child delivered. As time flies by, the babies grow into children and become integral members of the family, and the parents reshape their lives around those of their children.

The family nurtures interdependence

All people are born alone, however, in real life they all rely on one another. The family is the training ground for interdependence where members of the same family connect with one another on the basis of love, care, compassion and respect. As separate parts in a machine, when assembled, work together in harmony, so is the family when its members come together. Interdependence regarding real-life issues, such as helping the children in their education, sharing family chores or looking after one another when required, contributes to the physical, emotional and spiritual wellbeing of all family members. Such 'small' acts in any family are instrumental in establishing a moral compass in the family in increasingly individualised and bewildered modern societies.

The interdependence of family members may obviously give rise to some inconveniences and disagreements within the family, as the emotions or actions of one member can affect the others, but this is life's reality and one should not only learn to live with such inconveniences but also turn the latter's resulting challenges into joy and adventure. Basic compromise, giving preference to others and the individual members' significant autonomy are very important for establishing a positive interdependence within the family. Autonomy is critical as children enter their adolescent years with a great deal of confusion, uncertainty and an emerging newly-found sense of independence. Parents should hold their nerve at this stage and keep on guiding their children so that this does not lead to selfish individualism; their message should be loving and clear: 'yes, you are grown up individuals, but you are still invaluable members of the family'.

More often than not, once children leave their adolescent rebellious years behind, they realise that it was generally their parents who continually 'had their back'.

With the passage of time, the next phase that the family has to face is care for its elderly. In recent years, this has become big news with occasional national scandals reflecting dismal failure. 'Neglectful Britons blamed for forcing elderly into care homes', announced a headline[31] in one broadsheet in December 2012.

At the same time, the provision of services at nursing homes and hospices has been found to be inadequate in many places. As the number of elderly people increases, their abuse also keeps rising. General frailty, diseases associated with old age, such as dementia and emotional needs, demand long term palliative care. With the shrinking of the budget for health and social care, the gap between demand and supply is getting wider, which makes the abuse of the elderly also get worse.

---

31 http://www.telegraph.co.uk/news/uknews/9773652/Neglectful-Britons-blamed-for-forcing-elderly-into-care-homes.html

Caring families, value-laden societies and accountable states must work together to care for the elderly who deserve a dignified life and support in their last years. It is cruel for any civilised society to fail in providing adequate care for its senior citizens who gave so much to build it.

Dignity in caring for the elderly

Individualism and over-indulgence in today's commercialised societies have affected modern life and only very few people are immune from this. This has given rise to self-centred lifestyles in which the noble task of looking after the elderly is often shunned. Ageism is bringing occasional acts of disgrace even to societies where human rights are taken seriously. Civilised people are known for their noble treatment of the weak amongst them; a dignified society is expected to be at the service of its vulnerable elderly, including old-age pensioners. It is only sensible that one reciprocates an unending love and care towards those who bestowed on one the same when one was extremely fragile in early childhood. It is only a matter of time before it is one's turn to become old and frail.

While society and the state have a duty to care for the elderly and should have effective plans to address the issue of elderly care, families should be at the heart of this. Faith communities have religious-based moral teachings and varying degrees of know-how to care for the elderly; some have in-built institutions to address this matter. Parents and grandparents are venerated in most religious communities and children 'pay their debt' by being extra-loving to them and looking after their needs.

The humane treatment of the elderly is a virtuous circle and creates a win-win situation in the family; young children find an invaluable opportunity to learn from the knowledge and wisdom of their grandparents while the grandparents are saved from being bored due to loneliness and the inability to remain active. In the Islamic holy book, the

Qur'an, God mentions this reality concerning old age.[32] The following verses from the Qur'an[33] summarise, for adult Muslim children, the Islamic teachings on how to be respectful and tender towards their elderly parents, as their parents were once towards them.

> And your Lord has decreed that you not worship any but Him; and be good to your parents. If either or both of them reach old age with you, do not say to them 'fie'; and do not chide them, but speak to them a generous word. And be humble and tender to them and say, "My Lord, show mercy to them as they nurtured me when I was small."

---

32 He whom we bring unto old age, We reverse him in creation (weak, dependent and with little knowledge or ability to understand, like children). Will they then not understand? - (Qur'an, 36:68)
33 Qur'an, 17:23-24.

14

Being aware of children's online activities

Children of the present generation, particularly in the developed world, are fortunate in the sense that they can benefit from a number of things that the previous generations simply did not have, from state-of-the-art educational facilities to sophisticated technological gadgets that could barely have been imagined even two or three decades ago. One of the greatest inventions of the present time is the World Wide Web. The mere fact that information can be shared instantly in a number of ways across the globe is astonishing. One can use the internet, in a hand-held laptop or palm-held smartphone, to check one's ancestry for several centuries back, or perhaps research the credentials of an organisation for which one is applying for a job.

Benefits and harms

With these easily-accessible gadgets, the social media have now amazingly flourished and are affecting the personal and social lives of many adults and children in developed countries; the average weekly screen time has shot up significantly. It is reported[34] that average American adults say: 'we watch when we want, not when anyone tells us, and usually alone, and often while doing several other things. The sound bite has been replaced by virality, meme, hot take, tweet.' The fear is that, in such an environment, serious national issues cannot be realistically explored in any coherent and meaningful way.

Online activities seem great and cool to growing children who want to explore the world with a click of the button. This does have its own benefits as it enables friends to stay in regular contact with one another; it also facilitates the cultivation of relationships with people that are otherwise difficult to reach. Depending on their choice, they are also more aware of their chosen topics such as sports, economy and politics. Although aimed for slightly older students of around A-Level age, LinkedIn, for example enables aspiring young professionals to connect with one another to further and fulfil their career ambitions.

For average children, the possibilities are endless; it can be a wonderful educational tool that they are increasingly expected to use in their learning. However, it is this very fact that makes the internet a potentially dangerous tool. As children have now access to small devices, such as mobiles, watches and tablets, they can be in touch with a multitude of harmful or even dangerous sites and may watch pornography or be potentially targeted by cyber bullying or groomed for sex or radicalisation.

---

34 https://www.theguardian.com/media/2017/feb/02/amusing-ourselves-to-death-neil-postman-trump-orwell-huxley?utm_source=esp&utm_medium=E-mail&utm_campaign=GU+Today+main+NEW+H+categories&utm_term=211477&subid=16675586&CMP=EMCNEWEML6619I2.

British children aged between five to sixteen years spend an average of 6.5 hours a day[35] in front of TV screens, consoles, mobiles, computers and tablets. One startling fact that has emerged in recent years is that phones are no longer for talking to people. According to a 2016 Mobile Consumer Survey[36] carried out by Deloitte, 'almost half of 18-24 year olds check their phone in the middle of the night.' Worryingly, '31% of smartphone users make no traditional voice calls in any given week. This is contrasted with 25% in 2015, and just 4% in 2012.' If this continues, it will be 'the death of conversation'[37] with all what this entails of negative implications on human relationships.

It is for this very reason that parents, carers and teachers are extremely wary of how children use the internet, what they watch and with whom they communicate online. The prevalent norms among internet users are significantly shifting towards cyber-based customs and rituals. Children are growing up in an environment where there is less time for and emphasis on social interaction, even with friends in the playgrounds or parks. Lesser time for personal interaction with their near and dear ones at home, friends and the general public can negatively affect their communication skills.

At the same time, more online time means less physical movement, activities and exercise, which affects children's health as significant proportion of them are increasingly suffering from obesity.

The online world associated with social media platforms carries a number of potential dangers – one of which is cyber bullying, such as scandalous text messages, emails and postings on the likes of Facebook, which can destroy children's peace of mind and traumatise them. Bullying in schools is not new, but children using social media outlets turn them into powerful instruments to intimidate their victims and

35 http://www.dailymail.co.uk/sciencetech/article-3015293/Children-spent-six-hours-DAY-screens-likely-watch-shows-tablet-TV.html.
36 https://www2.deloitte.com/uk/en/pages/technology-media-and-telecommunications/articles/mobile-consumer-survey.html.
37 http://www.huffingtonpost.com/canon-jjohn/post_11389_b_9583856.html.

cause them to have suicidal thoughts. There is indeed a strong link between bullying and suicide. Bullying may start as a joke, but it can have a powerful effect on its target and cause educational and behavioural problems at school. Whether it is online, through the social media or texting, bullying is dangerous for children as it greatly affects their self-esteem and weakens them from inside. Rumours sent by email or posted on social networking sites and embarrassing pictures, videos or even fake profiles are also methods of cyber bullying. An estimated 160,000 children miss school every day due to their fear of being attacked or intimidated by other students.[38]

Another danger related to the web is the use of internet pornography. One lives today in an over-sexualised era where children are exposed to the opposite gender at an early age of their puberty when passion runs faster than reason. Kids nowadays reach puberty earlier than in previous generations and become sexually active at a quite tender age. Many children growing in lax family environments, with weak boundaries, are engaged in sexually explicit messages or photographs via mobile phone (sexting) in lower secondary schools. The sex market is continually thriving to the extent that children are, to a degree, expected to have physical relations with the opposite sex at their early teen years. This is a real worry for many parents and guardians today. The opposite sex is constantly objectified, not least through online pornography and the profit-seeking advertisement industry.

For children who are still impressionable in life, the lure of 'online dating', especially teen dating, for which there are easily available apps, is tremendous. Through this, children come across people they have never seen before and often exchange sexually explicit pictures that can be exploited to abuse them. As teens develop emotionally, they are heavily influenced by experiences in their relationships. Some, particularly girls, end up being sexually groomed by criminals. There have been far too many horror stories of how young girls undergo traumatic experiences, lose their way and even lives.

---

38 http://www.cyberbullyhotline.com/10-01-12-edtech-digest.html.

More poignant in these times is the great danger of online radicalisation and extremism. Some vulnerable children who may feel out of place in society or disenchanted with the authorities, but have little or skewed knowledge of their religion, get a 'sense of worth' through online slick propaganda of extremist or terrorist groups; more inquisitive children may find themselves connected to the dark webs. Online radicalisation can lure young people to glamorised violence and terrorism which not only destroy individuals and families but also put whole communities under "the Sword of Damocles". A number of young British Muslims did exactly this in recent years, when they joined terrorist groups such as Daesh (ISIL) and left everything behind to fight in faraway lands. This has been a heart-rending experience for their parents and communities.

Handling online activities effectively

The Prophet Muhammad (peace and blessings be upon him) said:

> *Allah (SWT) will ask every caretaker about the people under his care, and every man will be asked about the people of his household.* (Abū Dāwūd)

There must be effective strategies at home and in schools to grab the bull of online dangers by the horn. As a first step, parents should have basic knowledge of the web world and be aware of the shifting phase of social media that benefit people but potentially harm children. At the same time, they have to acknowledge that the propensity of today's children to use the internet, at home or in school, is a reality; the clock cannot be turned back. Parents should not put themselves as barriers in children's online learning; however, the harm latent in it should be kept at bay. They should rather help their children by sensitively monitoring, mentoring and coaching them in the proper use of the internet; they do not necessarily have to be expert in technology.

Positive and empathetic parenting generates healthy parents-children relationship that helps develop strong family values and a religious-cultural ethos in children. Relationship based on love, respect, values and mutual trust give children the confidence to discuss their feelings and the challenges they may face at school, in the streets and the social media. Positive body language and gestures as well as clear and consistent communication at home guarantee that children have trust in their parents and the responsible adults around them. A positive home environment, where parents sit and talk with their children, either one-to-one or in a family setting, helps in finding a common ground on agreed family rules, disciplined online use, etc.

One useful tip at home is to keep laptops or computers in a common area such as the living room or corridor so that children, before the age of responsibility, use them in the presence of others. In practising Muslim families, children are always taught to believe in the presence of a loving God. The fasting of the month of Ramadan trains the believers to stay away from food, drink and vulgarity. This spiritual training also affects children positively and helps them to stay away from harmful acts such as browsing unsafe websites. Parents can also consult their children and block certain undesirable sites or apps.

As technology today has become pervasive, parents should make their best judgment as to when their children are allowed to get certain electronic gadgets. Children's emotional and intellectual maturity and trustworthiness should always be taken into consideration. One option could be if, say, a child needs a mobile phone in primary school years, a simple set is given to him or her for just keeping in touch with home. As children grow and start going to secondary schools, which may be far from home, there should be honest and empathetic discussions with them regarding the controlled use of smartphones before they get them. Children are aware of their parents' love and worry for them, so they can understand why restricting their use of the internet is needed for their own benefit.

In an age dominated by online social media, where children can be tempted by the glamour of the virtual world, parents should create a loving, caring and compassionate home environment through personal relationship and effective communication within the family. When physical interaction is not possible, the next best option is video communication through apps such as FaceTime and Skype. There are many video apps that can now be used for free. Personal interaction and video communication help improve parents-children relationship. When video facilities are not available, audio communication should be the next option, for at least voices are heard; one can at least feel one's interlocutor's presence and change of tone. Text communication, which is impersonal, should be used as and when needed, but it should never take over other means of communication.

15

Safeguarding one's children from harm

Children in all cultures are seen as a blessing and an invaluable gift. The family and home are at the centre of children's safety and overall wellbeing. The local authorities have an overarching responsibility[39] to safeguard and promote the welfare of all children and young people in their areas. But the police, children's social care and the NSPCC (National Society for the Prevention of Cruelty to Children) are the relevant agencies that have statutory powers to protect, safeguard and promote the welfare of children in the UK. Parents and other adults in organisations, such as schools, youth centres and religious institutions that work with children, have an obligation to be aware of and report concerns related to children protection and the safeguarding of young people under the age of 18.

---

39 https://www.gov.uk/government/uploads/system/uploads/attachment_data/file/592101/Working_Together_to_Safeguard_Children_20170213.pdf.

Child safeguarding means more than 'child protection' and relates to the action taken to promote the welfare of children and protecting them from harm. Safeguarding is everyone's responsibility and is defined as: 'protecting children from maltreatment; preventing the impairment of children's health or development; ensuring that children grow up in circumstances consistent with the provision of safe and effective care; and taking action to enable all children to have the best outcomes.' Safeguarding includes protecting children from all harms, including online sexual grooming and radicalisation. Safeguarding arrangements can only be effective if a children-centred approach is adopted, since a clear understanding of the needs and views of children is vital.

Child Protection is about protecting children from abuse.[40] There are four categories of child protection issues in the UK:

Physical abuse: According to the World Health Organisation, this means intentional use of physical force that results in or can cause harm to the child's health, survival, development or dignity. This includes hitting, kicking, shaking, strangling, scalding, poisoning and suffocating – sometime with the intention of punishing the child.

Sexual abuse: This refers to involving a child in a sexual act aimed toward physical gratification or financial profit and pressuring a child to engage in sexual activities or indecent exposure.

Psychological abuse: According to the American Psychological Association, this means non-accidental verbal or symbolic acts by parents, caregivers or adults that result or can result in significant psychological harm to the child.

---

40 Preventing Child Maltreatment: a guide to taking action and generating evidence, World Health Organisation and International society for Prevention of Child Abuse and Neglect, 2006.

Neglect: This refers to the failure of a parent or carer to provide needed food, clothing, shelter, medical care or supervision. It is also refers to lack of attention, love and nurturing from the adults around the child.

A child can experience multiple abuses over a period of time and this can happen online. Over half a million children are abused in the UK every year.[41] Parenting demands a reasonable awareness of the nature of abuse children can go through in institutions such as schools as well as online.

The Government's Prevent strategy and Muslim children

From 1 July 2015, schools are bound under section 26 of the Counter-Terrorism and Security Act (CTSA) 2015 to have 'due regard to the need to prevent people from being drawn into terrorism.' Known as the Prevent duty,[42] this applies to a wide range of public-facing bodies and their purpose is to keep children safe from the risk of radicalisation and extremism. The safeguarding of children now includes keeping them safe from the harm of radicalisation. The terms radicalisation and extremism have specific meanings in the context of Prevent; the former is the process by which a person comes to support terrorism and extremist ideologies associated with terrorist groups; the latter means vocal or active opposition to fundamental British values, including democracy, the rule of law, individual liberty and mutual respect and tolerance of different faiths and beliefs. Extremism also includes calling for the death of members of the armed forces.

Since the 7/7 London bombings, radicalisation and extremism have become associated mostly with Muslims; a series of counter-

---

41 https://www.nspcc.org.uk/preventing-abuse/child-abuse-and-neglect/

42 https://www.gov.uk/government/uploads/system/uploads/attachment_data/file/439598/prevent-duty-departmental-advice-v6.pdf

terrorism measures since then created a sense of unease in the Muslim community as many felt they, and their youth in particular, have been disproportionately seen through the prism of security. The debate has continued until today.

The CTSA 2015 has put a stronger emphasis on the Government's existing Channel Programme which is an early multi-agency intervention process designed to safeguard vulnerable people from being drawn to violent extremist or terrorist behaviour. The expectation is that the local authorities, nurseries, schools, universities, social services, healthcare services, the criminal justice system and the police more or less anyone involved in the care and development of young people monitor people for signs of extremism and refer them to the relevant panels.

This has already created a difficult situation in the education sector. One east London school was said to have used 'anti-radicalisation software' in the last summer to monitor pupils and offered workshops for parents on spotting signs of radicalisation amongst small children. In another case, five primary schools with a large number of Muslim pupils in a London Borough asked pupils to complete surveys designed to provide clues as to who is most susceptible to possible radicalisation. Many, including some head teachers, expressed concerns at this bizarre methodology.

The primary focus of parents of early-year children is about their children's overall growth through playing and learning activities to communicate, socialise and enjoy their childhood or about their children's safety from potential harms, such as bullying, etc. – not radicalisation at that tender age!

Most teachers are amazing professionals who come to the profession in order to share their talents and help prepare future generations of innovators and entrepreneurs. The question which imposes itself is: are teachers well-equipped, or do they have enough time, to deal with the extra burden of monitoring children who have started exploring their lives at school? Many experts feel that this is the task of the already established education welfare service and, on more serious matters, the police. Diverting teachers' time and energy to something that they are not particularly skilled to deal with is seen by many as ineffective.

A school is a place for promoting curiosity, critical thinking and creative expression, as well as harnessing the potentials of the young ones in their formative period. Schools are also for supporting children of local communities or groups that suffer from unequal opportunity so that each child is given the best chance to lead a successful life. The growing emphasis on security in the education sector may hamper the huge progress made by some, otherwise deprived, groups, such as the Bangladeshi and Pakistani communities, over the last two decades. With higher university intakes from these communities, which is not yet reflected in the job market or social mobility, many children from minority communities are showing greater confidence in a pluralist Britain and contributing to the nation. So, many Muslims and some experts in the wider society feel that this extra focus on young Muslim children is unfair and may jeopardise their progress and overall wellbeing.

The Muslim community fully supports safeguarding children from harm. But as Prevent has failed to get a buy-in from most people in it, many are confused; and this is not helping children's progress. It is mentioned that Prevent has been successful in some areas; however, on enquiry it was found that the local authorities have been applying it sensitively with the help of the community and the term Prevent was rarely used in relation to safeguarding children.

The elephant in the room is how extremism is defined and what causes young people to leave everything behind to join some barbaric cults in the name of religion that defy religious teachings and basic human rights. There are obviously multiple factors for this in a pluralist and commercialised environment, such as social deprivation, lack of trust in the authorities, grievances against inequality and injustice, prejudice or discrimination, ignorance or skewed readings of religious texts, mental health, slick online propaganda for violence, etc. Adolescence is challenging and young people who suffer from hopelessness or anger issues may be attracted to drugs, criminality, extremism or violence.

There is no denying the fact that a section of young people in the Muslim community, however small and for whatever reasons, has problems with radicalisation and extremism. One is also seeing now an increasing far-right political rhetoric that is exacerbating extremism in some parts of Europe. This constitutes a nightmare for parents!

On the issues of addressing radicalisation and extremism, a two-fold approach is needed. On the one hand a meaningful conversation with communities has to be launched and a national strategy devised in order to find a comprehensive solution to the problem. On the other, an intellectually sound and evidence-based grass-roots approach to de-radicalisation must be put forward by targeting vulnerable individuals. Parents from all communities should raise their game at home and in their neighbourhoods to ensure their children's proper safeguard from all harms.

16

Assisting one's grown-up children in their marriage

The Muslim communities in Britain are going through generational changes. The new generations are gradually shaping the dynamics of their own communities by bringing in more energy and professionalism as well as some challenges. They are generally more confident in engaging with, and contributing to, the wider society in various ways. The overall picture is mixed; there are success stories in some areas of life, but there are also areas that need huge improvements.

The presence of a growing number of educated middle class young Muslims, belonging to Generation M (as one author calls them),[43] who are 'proud of their faith, enthusiastic consumers, dynamic, engaged,

---

43 https://www.theguardian.com/world/2016/sep/03/meet-generation-m-the-young-affluent-muslims-changing-the-world.

creative and demanding' is now felt in 21st century Britain. However, a large proportion of ordinary young people from the Muslim community are still struggling with a disadvantaged, socio-economic condition, on the one hand, and post-7/7 scrutiny alongside prejudice and lack of social mobility, on the other.

Young Muslims today are in many ways different from their parents' generation. Like their peers in the wider society, sometimes referred to pejoratively as Generation Snowflake,[44] they are more prone to taking offence and more emotionally vulnerable vis-à-vis life's challenges; they also lack resilience and are known to be more afflicted with mental health problems.

Whether highflying or struggling for the basics, the parents' love for their grown-up children knows no bound. This love is embedded in well-defined obligations and moral responsibilities in any family setup. In Islamic culture and Muslim traditions, the parents have a responsibility to discuss the issues of career and marriage with their grown-up children; children are also accustomed to this. Careers, jobs and marriage are issues that always need wise counselling from close trustworthy people who have better experience and wisdom in life. Depending on the home environment or traditions sustaining it, young people go through some cultural, moral and spiritual education with reasonable boundaries to allow them to navigate positively through contemporary social norms. Successful youths develop self-esteem, confidence and social competence – although some may struggle in making sense of their lives in a secular and pluralist milieu. However, the parents have to be sensitive in ensuring that their counselling is not seen as overbearing.

Getting a suitable job, especially in the public sector, in a post-9/11 world is tougher for young Muslims. Although Britain is meritocratic and is known to be far better than other European countries, as far as equal opportunities are concerned, Muslims face some challenges when

---

44 https://en.wikipedia.org/wiki/Generation_Snowflake.

it comes to better jobs and social mobility. In spite of the Equality Act 2010, the BBC has recently found[45] that a job seeker with an English-sounding name is likely to be offered three times the number of interviews than an applicant with a Muslim name. When it comes to managerial and professional occupations, the situation is even worse.[46]

Marriage and the parents' contribution

In most faith communities, particularly the Muslim community, the importance of a marriage-based family is over-arching. Marriage at a right age between two matured and responsible man and woman is considered a blessing. It is a powerful antidote against reckless and transitory boy-girl relationships. The believers consider a happy marital life an essential ingredient for a successful life in this world and the hereafter.

Marriage links young adults with the deep-rooted human tradition of building a family on the basis of mutual rights and obligations. It gives young people mental peace or tranquillity (*Arabic: Sakīnah*), an emotional anchor and spiritual solace. The believer cannot remain celibate without a genuine and valid reason. Some people suggest, and experience dictates, that the best age for getting married is around twenty-five, although there may be other factors that contribute in getting married before or after such an age range.

Boys and girls who are raised in positive family environments learn to interact with one another naturally and decently in the public domain in educational institutions or workplaces – by maintaining a respectable and safe distance between them. The inner strength of their character is vital for their spiritual journey. In accordance with the Islamic teachings, men and women in post-puberty period, who are not "closely related" (*Arabic: Maḥram*), never meet with each other in

---

45 http://www.bbc.co.uk/news/uk-england-london-38751307.
46 https://www.demos.co.uk/project/rising-to-the-top/.

seclusion (*Arabic: Khalwah*).[47] The purpose of this apparently 'strict' regime in man-woman relationship is to protect their chastity.

Marriage in Islam is a Prophetic *Sunnah*. Like many other things in life, Islam has its guidelines for young people when choosing marriage partners – the *dīn* or religiosity is the over-arching quality they should look for when they choose a spouse. In a *ḥadīth*, related by a number of authorities, the Prophet (peace and blessings be upon him) said that, through marriage, a person completes half of his or her religion.[48]

Marriage is a serious business; young people should not be driven to it by impulse, transient attraction or outward looks. The outward features of the future spouse should not be discarded, but young aspiring men or women should endeavour to look deep into their future partners' inner qualities and backgrounds. The consequences of choosing a wrong marriage partner lead to frustration and failure in life. Choosing a spouse, another independent human being with a different background, should not be taken lightly. Young morally upright people obviously look for morally upright spouses and make extra efforts for this purpose by seeking advice about finding a suitable match.

In light of the decline in marriage and increasing divorce rates in modern times, parents feel more obligated to help their beloved sons and daughters in finding suitable spouses. Responsible parents must get involved in the marriages of their children and not just sit passively and moan about their helplessness regarding this matter. They have a moral right to see that their beloved ones do not make mistakes when choosing their life partners. Sensible parents can realistically help their post-adolescent, adult children, if they had raised them in an open family environment with love and respect. Close and loving family members usually help in this matter through frank and polite discussions.

---

47 Whenever a man sits with a woman in privacy, a third one always creeps in, and that is the *Shayṭān* (the devil) (al-Tirmidhī)
48 When Allah's servant marries he has completed one half of the Religion. Thereafter let him fear Allah regarding the remaining half. (al-Bayhaqī)

Sensible young adults also look up to their parents and other close experienced people, such as friends or mentors, for guidance before choosing their spouses. They see marriage as a sacred institution for the continuity of life and wellbeing of society.

Of course, adult sons or daughters ought not to be coerced to get married; 'forced marriage' has nothing to do with the Muslim tradition. The Prophet of Islam annulled marriage contracts that were conducted under duress. On the other hand, the rejection or avoidance of the parents' contribution to their marriage is also alien to the Islamic tradition.

In the Islamic tradition, a young man needs to have basic financial earnings before he can start a family. However, both men and women should be mentally and emotionally ready. When choosing a spouse, the believers are advised to give priority to religiosity[49] over other considerations. Other considerations, such as education, are also important. Young adults are advised to discuss and clarify their views and expectations regarding their future marital life. Not only should sensible, young Muslim adults try to find out whether or not they are on the same page with their prospective spouses, they should also check whether they share a similar attitude towards life. Moreover, practising Muslims perform the prayer of *Istikhārah*[50] regarding any important issue in their lives, such as choosing life-partners.

Marriage is one thing, but sustaining it with love, care and compassion is another. After marriage, as couples wake up from the world of pre-marriage idealism to face post-marriage realism, they may encounter challenges and ups and downs in their relationship. Like any close human relationship, marriage is not free from hiccups. Marriage in Islam, which is also a social contract involving two families, can give

---

49 'A woman is married for four things: her wealth, her beauty, her lineage or her *dīn*. Always choose a woman for her *dīn*.' (*Ṣaḥīḥ al-Bukhārī*, Muslim, Abū Dāwūd and al-Nasā'ī)

50 *Istikhārah* – a prayer performed by Muslims when in need of guidance from God on an important issue in their lives. 'None fails who consults (others) and none regrets who seeks (God's) choice.' Al-Ṭabarānī

rise to contentious issues with the in-laws. Sensible newly-wed couples should be aware of such dynamics beforehand, plan ahead to minimise foreseeable tensions and learn how to handle any difficult situation. In-laws from both sides should also control their behaviour; they must not interfere with the lives of newly-married couples, for cultural or any other reason. They should rather positively add to the new family's synergy and help it to develop.

In most cultures the parents' responsibility never ends; it only changes in nature and level, until the parents leave this world. Whether or not the parents and their newly-married children live under the same roof, the parents have a moral duty to provide sound advice to their adult children. However, the coercive and intrusive involvement in their children's marital life, witnessed in some cultures even today, is unhelpful and unacceptable. On the other hand, children should always express their gratitude and show humility to their parents – particularly, when they become frail. This is an inevitable cycle of life. Educated and enlightened young people never miss out on their parents' company and wisdom. In a loving family environment, each generation has a unique role to play.

17

Family, faith and the future

The shooting of 29-year-old Mark Duggan by armed police in north London on the evening of 4 August 2011 was followed by riots, looting and mayhem in London and, subsequently, other English cities – carried out mostly by youths. The first human casualties of this were three Asian Muslim young men in Birmingham who were defending their properties.

Such wanton destruction up and down the country by sections of young men, mostly with the help of the social media, was seen as a sign of a social malaise which caused concern in the country. There was a universal revulsion at the riots' mind-boggling anarchy and mindless criminality. Columnist Peter Oborne commented,[51] that 'the moral decay at the top of society was as bad as at the bottom.

---

51 https://www.opendemocracy.net/ourkingdom/peter-oborne/moral-decay-of-british-society-is-as-bad-at-top-as-bottom.

Amidst widespread pessimism, as the whole country was longingly waiting for the London Olympics and Paralympics the following year (2012), some citizens displayed inspirational examples of bravery and feelings for their fellow citizens. Local residents in some places fought back the looters and self-retrained vigilantes joined the police forces to help protect properties and the streets; ordinary Londoners were seen cleaning their streets after each major disturbance. Indeed, faith played an important role, particularly for Muslims, as it was the month of Ramadan the fasting of which emphasises restraint and shunning evil and criminal activities. Muslims and many others chased the looters and the Turkish shopkeepers in north London created a shield to protect their stores.

This led the editor of *Youthwork* magazine to write an optimistic piece[52] in which he mentioned, 'my faith-based youth work gives me hope in this generation.' In a powerful article, the writer A N Wilson eulogised[53] the father of two dead young sons for his 'solemn, peaceful message that will make everyone who stereotypes Muslims as terrorists and fanatics feel ashamed of themselves.' I wrote a piece on the importance of the family[54] in raising good human beings and citizens; family and faith, to me, are vital for the reconstruction of society, even if it happens to be a secular one!

What was it that caused this sheer criminality and nihilism in certain sections of British youth? The issues had always been complex and there is no simple answer. Many causes were cited: the widening socio-economic inequality; the decline of trust in the established authorities (such as politicians, bankers and media bosses); the unrestricted commercialisation of life; the gradual waning of the moral compass with a 'me-first' philosophy of life; the weakening of the family structure

---

52 https://www.theguardian.com/commentisfree/belief/2011/aug/12/riots-faith-based-youth-work.
53 https://www.google.co.uk/webhp?sourceid=chrome-instant&ion=1&espv=2&ie=UTF-8#q=A+N+Wilson.
54 http://www.huffingtonpost.co.uk/muhammad-abdul-bari/family-should-be-at-the-h_b_929364.html.

which caused a lack of values and discipline at home, in schools and the streets. All these cited causes are relevant to varying degrees.

Fortunately the country pulled together during the summer of 2012 and the Brits had the most successful Olympics and Paralympics ever without any hiccups.

Young people are the makers or breakers of any society; they are the future. The society that has a robust family structure, strong family values and positive parenting can easily turn the energy of its youths into an element of nation building. If the above-mentioned positive factors are weak, they can become a recipe for the kind of disorder that one witnessed in the 2011 summer riots. One must build strong and cohesive families, have faith in the youth and raise them through proactive and positive parenting in all the nation's communities – those of faith and those of no-faith.

Young people are naturally creative, adventurous and prone to challenging authority or even rebel against it. They brim with energy and are natural idealists. At the same time, they are impressionable and often vulnerable. Without a strong moral anchor, primarily coming from the family and faith, they may enter the adult world ill-prepared. Their tendency to challenge the status quo is natural, so without a strong but positive discipline that begins in their childhood at home, with age-appropriate freedom, young people may easily lose out in life. They may turn out to be difficult or even 'problem children'. Schools are often at the sharp end of juvenile indiscipline and delinquency. They may be blown away with confusion and frustration due to generational and cultural gaps with their parents and the mixed signals they may get from their family and society in childhood. Increasing uncertainty in the parents' authority on their children is another area which can cause confusion about the limits set for disciplining children.

I have worked with secondary school-aged children and their parents since the early 1990s. I believe that the family is at the heart of children's secure and promising lives. The most important reason for children's indiscipline and delinquency is to be found in their homes, their families. However, pointing all the fingers at the parents for their children's negative behaviours is not entirely justified; everyone shares the responsibility of this state of affairs.

Children start their lives at home. A warm, caring and stable family environment is essential for children's healthy growth. No society can survive for long with a weak family structure, even if such a statement may seem old-fashioned, traditional, or even judgemental. Human society stands on the shoulder of its families. Strong families create strong moral values, such as love, respect, care, patience, sacrifice, integrity, openness and compromise. Successful families nurture a culture of consultation and problem solving. But all this depends on an assertive, proactive and positive parenting from the early stages of children's lives. According to a survey[55] conducted by YouGov for Channel 4/ITN after the summer 2011 riots, the British people thought that poor parenting, criminal behaviour and gang culture were causing unrest in cities across the UK.

This change in social reality worries the people of faith as well as many others. The weakening of the institution of marriage is also a major concern. This may raise eyebrows amongst many people in modern developed societies, as the very idea of marriage, traditional family values and the parents' role are seen as signs of backwardness. But one must not forget that these are at the heart of society and must not be brushed aside. Without a delicate balance in the family and social life, one may go down the slippery slope of creating incurable social problems.

Like life's other realities, a marriage-based family is not trouble-free. But as the oldest of human institutions, it has been the cornerstone of society. Through the extended family structure in the past and nuclear families in modern times, the parents and their children build a unique and basic organisation in society. With mothers generally at the centre, families give hope in despair, solace in grief and strength in frailty.

---

55 https://www.channel4.com/news/poor-parenting-to-blame-for-uk-riots-says-exclusive-poll.

As marriage between a man and a woman is rooted in religious orthodoxy, it has some simple procedures. Marriage demands a committed relationship between the spouses, with joint responsibilities towards their children. Other families and the community as a whole are also included in the joy of starting this new journey by two newly-wed people.

However, the family structure is coming under a lot of pressure as the importance of marriage is being significantly undermined. Co-habitation without marriage and children born out of wedlock are becoming widespread; this has overturned the social stigma that was once attached to relationships outside marriage.

In post-modern lifestyles in developed countries, the relationship between a man and a woman is often transitory, fluid and informal. In the absence of any social contract or social pressure, marriage between couples can be easily broken. Changing partners is becoming more common. The arrival of children may delay or halt the breakage of a relationship, but fidelity may be compromised. Additionally, as children from previous relationships become involved in such complications, the situation can become even more complex with multiple relationships brought together in a blended or step family – mum, dad, mum's partner and close family members, dad's partner and close family members – and the list goes on. Increased tension, emotions and disputes can affect children's smooth upbringing. For some adult men and women, blended families may be adventurous, but it is likely that their children will grow with disadvantages compared to other children of families where the mother and father have formed a stable relationship.

Experience shows that frequent changes of partners, without any deep commitment or meaningful responsibility towards one another, is one of the main reasons for an increasing number of 'problem children' in many developed countries. This has an impact on the quality of school education with even a higher social and economic cost. This is a huge worry for many parents, educationalists and social scientists.

Whatever the type of the family, abuse or neglect always has an adverse effect on children. With unrestricted consumerism and the arrival of modern electronic gadgets, people are drifting further apart and parents' quality time with their children is being gradually reduced. In worse cases, this is putting extra pressures on the NHS, the police and the social services.

British social trends have changed over the decades. The number of marriages has hit an all-time low in recent years. Fewer people are getting married since the figures of marriage were recorded in 1895. Additionally, the average marriage age has also gone up; British women are now marrying late. In 2011, their average marriage age was 30, compared to 25.5 in 1991. The same applies to men; their average marriage age was 32.1 in 2009, compared to 25.4 in 1981.

There are no reliable figures for marriage in faith communities. But it is believed that there is a domino effect of this social trend on all communities. Although marriage remains a solid institution for orthodox religious groups, the average age of marriage has risen for most religious communities, including Muslims. I have observed that the average age of marriage for Muslim men and women, especially from the educated middle class, has risen sharply. Careerism, the change of lifestyle, unrealistic expectations from the spouses and the increasing costs of weddings may be contributing factors.

Due to prevailing social trends, people are becoming increasingly individualistic and, thus, they fail to live in compromise with their near and dear ones. Consumerism is eating away at people's desire for long term, higher objectives in life. Over-sexualisation is also adversely affecting balance in gender relations. The rights of the parents, such as instilling a moral anchor in their children, are getting ignored.

Humans have made unprecedented scientific and technological progress in recent decades, but at the same time their moral compass is dwindling, with many social norms thrown into the wind. 'Our scientific power has outrun our spiritual power. We have guided missiles and misguided men', said Martin Luther King Junior many decades ago. What people need is a spiritual anchor and the age-old tradition of holding together in families, neighbourhoods and communities.

18

Instilling awareness in one's children about human equality

Islam's emphasis on human equality and the current Muslim reality

The shocking killing of George Floyd in the US on 25th May sparked global protests and reignited discussions on human equality and redressing the dark heritage of European colonialism and slave trade.

The COVID-19 pandemic and the lockdown it has forced upon people have also driven some conscientious Muslims to reflect on racism as well as some less discussed and understated prejudices within Muslim communities.

It is ironic that an egalitarian religion like Islam, in which racism was sharply nipped in the bud by none other than the Prophet Muhammad (peace and blessings be upon him), still has followers who harbour hidden, or not-so-hidden, racist views. Beneath the beautiful displays of equality in congregational prayers or the pilgrimage, the attitude and dealings of some Muslims towards others, who are of a supposedly 'inferior' ethnicity, clan, colour or class, is nothing short of a disgrace. Like structural or systemic racism embedded in western countries, discreet racism is alive and kicking in sections of Muslim communities.

Additionally, the treatment of migrant labourers in some Arab countries is no less disgraceful. Under a system that simulates modern slavery, a migrant worker's immigration status is legally bound to an individual employer or *kafil* (sponsor) for the duration of his contract. Verbal, physical, sexual and psychological mistreatments of migrant workers, irrespective of their religion, have been reported under this *kafālah* system. These workers are often denied the right to address the violation of their rights while domestic workers are confined within the homes of their sponsors, which makes them very vulnerable.

Islam, on the other hand, clearly demands of Muslims to firmly believe in *Tawḥīd*, or the oneness of God the Almighty, which sows the seeds of human equality and respect in their hearts. The Qur'an (49:13) declares that all humans have originated from the same father and mother and that race and colour have no consequence whatsoever in the eyes of God: *"O mankind! We created you from a single (pair) of a male and a female and made you into nations and tribes that you may know or recognise each other. Verily the most honoured of you in the sight of Allah is the one who is the most righteous of you..."* In his last sermon, the Prophet Muhammad (peace and blessings be upon him) declared: 'All mankind is from Adam and Eve, an Arab has no superiority over a non-Arab nor a non-Arab over an Arab; and a white person has no superiority over a black person nor a black person over a white person, unless it be for piety and good action.'

"Our master emancipated our master"

The second rightly-guided caliph 'Umar expressed his respect for Bilāl ibn Rabāḥ (a freed black slave chosen as Islam's first *muezzin* by the Prophet) in a unique manner when he said: 'Abū Bakr is our master and he emancipated our master'. *(Ṣaḥīḥ al-Bukhārī)* In choosing Bilāl for this dignified role, the Prophet demonstrated the social inclusion of all the believers regardless of their background at a time when slavery and racism were systemic in society. Muslims proudly use this example as evidence of their hatred of racism, but the thoughts and actions of some Muslims often belie this. Bilāl's story is a constant reminder that racism has no place in Islam. However, the existence of racism in some Muslim communities should be pointed out in order to rectify the attitudes and practices of some Muslims in real life.

Although Islam defeated racism and class prejudice, what is less known is that Bilāl did encounter prejudices from some Companions of Prophet Muhammad (peace and blessings be upon him). All Muslims should consider the beautiful manner whereby the Prophet wasted no time in correcting their wrongdoings. On one occasion the Prophetic Companion Abū Dharr al-Ghifārī insulted Bilāl by saying, "O son of a black woman". Bilāl was deeply hurt by this insult. Upon hearing this, the Prophet told Abū Dharr in a sad and firm tone that he still had remnants of pre-Islamic *jāhiliyah* (pagan ignorance) in him. Abū Dharr felt so ashamed that he ran to Bilāl and put his head on the sand, telling Bilāl to step on it as an expiation for his profane behaviour. Bilāl raised Abū Darr's head and kissed him on the cheek instead, showing his love and kindness to Abū Dharr. These two Companions and others like them belonged to what the Prophet (peace and blessings be upon him) called 'the best community'. Bilāl would later become the governor of Syria.

The life of Bilāl serves as a reminder to all Muslims that human status and dignity lie in piety and character, not in colour, class or race. They must also all be aware of the dangers of prejudice that can affect anyone, including Muslims, wittingly or unwittingly.

Class or caste-based prejudice
This is known to be prevalent amongst South Asian people, including Muslims, though it is by no means an exclusively South Asian issue.

More than two-third of the British Muslim population are South Asians. Class or caste-based prejudice is often brazenly exhibited by some Muslim institutions and families, especially when it comes to choosing marriage partners. In the name of maintaining *kafā'ah* (parity, equivalence or family match), the colour, caste or clan of marriageable boys and girls - rather than their education, piety and character - sometimes become determining factors. Amongst some Muslims in diaspora communities, the terms *farsha* (fair skin) and *kala* (dark skin), as well as family lineage of, say, Syeds or Chowdhurys, can create huge tensions within and between families.

Caste-based hierarchies, imported from ancient Indian Hindu culture, often rear their ugly heads even today. Towards the end of British colonialism, Bengali Muslims were seen as inferior by upper-caste Kolkata-based Hindu elites, even to the extent of questioning their Bengali ethnic identity. At the same time, Hindu upper-caste elites in India, hyped up by the Hindutva mentality, tended to treat Indian Muslims as Dalit Muslims. Dalits are the lower caste people who were often referred to as 'untouchables' in the Hindu social pecking order. Dr Ambedkar, an undisputed leader of India's Dalits and its great statesman, said that 'untouchability [is] worse than slavery.'

One British social observer wrote that anti-Blackness isn't just about the N-word, 'it's the aunt who judges people on the fairness of their skin or the uncle who blindly uses the term kala.' Sadly, caste-based prejudice has infiltrated the minds of many South Asian Muslims because of their proximity to Hindu culture. The fact that a distinction is still made between the *ashrāf* (Arabic word for those of Prophetic descent) and the non-*ashrāf amongst many* Asian Muslims flies in the face of basic Islamic values and human brotherhood.

Conclusion

Black people have suffered the most during different stages of human history because of their skin colour and they should not be referred to as 'just former slaves' in any public discourse. Islamic history is rich in its tradition of protecting those who are racially persecuted, from the lineage of one of the sons of Prophet Nūḥ, to kings like the Negus of Abyssinia who sheltered Muslims and protected them from the persecution of the pagans of Makkah in the early years of Islam. He also converted to Islam at the time of the Prophet Muhammad (peace and blessings be upon him).

Martin Luther King led the black civil rights movement which challenged white supremacy in America in the 1960s. There was also a parallel but radical tradition of challenging racism by none other than Malcolm X and Muhammad Ali, two global Muslim icons.

The #BlackLivesMatter movement has created a global consciousness about the historic and ongoing prejudice, discrimination and injustice that black people as well as other non-white minorities in the West suffer from. Simultaneously, this has also led conscientious people to seriously question the obscene socio-economic inequality existing in multicultural Britain.

It is time for Muslims from all backgrounds to rise above cultural baggage that is often embedded in prejudice. Racism cannot be ended with just rhetoric, quotes from the Qur'an or references from Islam's history. Muslims should be willing to listen, understand and reflect on the suffering of their fellow human beings before transferring their enlightened ethos to the next generation of British Muslims who belong to a different mind-set. What makes people dignified as stewards of Allah on this beautiful planet are only their actions and nothing else.

Muslim parents should educate their children about the legacy of their golden history and invest in creating a positive environment at home and in the mosques and community bodies. Only then will Muslim children grow up as mature adults with decent moral character traits, values of egalitarianism and respect for other human beings. Racism, whether hidden or not, is a scar on humanity and it must be called out wherever it is found.

Conclusion

Children open their eyes in this world and find unfathomable love from mum, dad and the adults around them. The family being at the heart of their secured and promising life, children's growth, as balanced human beings with unlimited potentials, starts at home. Living in a fast changing social environment, with a myriad of opportunities but also challenges, the parents need full concentration and creative energy in raising their children. Parenting is a full time job to help children grow physically, emotionally and intellectually until they become responsible adults.

Some of the issues discussed in this book are more pertinent in the present time: The rise in domestic abuse in recent decades is a real concern, as it is linked with other problems such as mental health, school discipline and criminality. And although young people have easy access to knowledge, thanks to an exponential technological progress, they are exposed to the misuse and overuse of technology. If children's surrounding environment is not based on compassion and respect, then the all-pervading modern individualism and consumerism will affect them from an early age. One is already observing a generation of loners who are physically inactive, with less connection with the people around them or the realities of this world, because they are often glued to the online world.

There is no easy solution to this modern reality; however, a stable and loving family accompanied by quality time between parents and their offspring as well as a proactive engagement with children is vital for them to acquire self-esteem, confidence and social activity for the common good. A higher level of responsibility, sense of urgency and consistency in efforts from parents and carers are now more needed than ever. There is no substitute to the parents' relationship with their children and the consistent use of a smart, non-threatening discipline regime at home. Irrespective of the parents' educational level, their close relationships with and disciplining of their children will help bridge generational and cultural gaps in the family. Moreover, children must be listened to; they want to be valued.

The parents' love for their children is immeasurable. For the people of faith, timeless religious teachings and natural role modelling in the family and the community are sources of motivation for young people. Examples are always better than precepts. In caring families, parents never shy away from lending a hand to their children throughout all the important phases of their lives, even when they become adults, such as helping them to select a suitable career and choose a spouse. In the Islamic tradition, the parents are expected to be 'friendly' with their children beyond the age of 14, although without exactly being like friends.

In spite of the challenges they faced upon starting life in in the UK in the 1970s and 1980s with socio-economic disadvantages, British Muslims have done significantly well for their children's education in the last two decades. With increasingly higher proportion of British born parents raising third or fourth generation children, it is vital they now turn much of their attention to improving their social mobility through various ways, such as social activism and civic participation. This should be accompanied by educational activities: reading, learning, reflecting and reasoning, as well as establishing creative enterprises for young Muslims to connect them with their forefathers' history and legacy that once helped European Renaissance. This will improve their rootedness in European soil as people of faith from the Abrahamic tradition. Through conscious efforts, they can raise a dynamic generation that is competent enough to take on the challenges of negative stereotypes and be a force for good for the whole society.

What can be more pleasurable than seeing one's offspring succeed in life? For people of faith, raising their innocent children to become righteous adults is also linked to acquiring eternal bliss. The Prophet Muhammad (peace and blessings be upon him) said: 'When a child of Adam dies all his or her deeds are cut off, with three exceptions: charity whose benefit is continuous, knowledge from which benefit is continuously reaped, or his or her righteous child making supplication for him or her'. (*Ṣaḥīḥ* Muslim)

Index